Green Line 2

Vorschläge zur Leistungsmessung

von
Martina Angele
Pauline Ashworth
Elise L. Köhler-Davidson
Simone Nothelle-Woters

Ernst Klett Verlag
Stuttgart · Leipzig

Liebe Lehrerin, lieber Lehrer,

die *Green Line* 2 Vorschläge zur Leistungsmessung orientieren sich an den Anforderungen für die Leistungsfeststellung.
Wie Sie wissen, legen die neuen Lehrpläne ganz besonderen Wert auf Kompetenzorientiertheit und kommunikativen Anspruch. Darauf haben wir bei der Entwicklung dieses Hefts geachtet, um Ihnen Aufgabenformate an die Hand zu geben, die auf dem neuesten Stand sind und sich daher optimal für die Erstellung von Klassenarbeiten eignen.
Bei der Entwicklung der kompetenzorientierten Aufgaben wurde besonderer Wert auf die Einbettung in für die Schüler aus dem Alltag bekannte Situationen gelegt.

Aufbau

Im **Kompetenzteil** finden Sie Aufgaben zu den fünf Kompetenzen Hörverstehen, Leseverstehen, Schreiben, Sprechen und Sprachmittlung. Da Sie alle Aufgaben editierbar auf der Lehrersoftware finden, können Sie diese beliebig und abgestimmt auf das Niveau Ihrer Klasse zu einer Klassenarbeit zusammenstellen.
So können z.B. Vorgaben reduziert oder ganz entfernt und Teilaufgaben gewählt werden. Zudem zeigt Ihnen das ⎍-Symbol an, dass es sich um eine vergleichsweise anspruchsvollere Aufgabe handelt.

Für die Speaking-Aufgaben sollte den SchülerInnen Zeit zur Vorbereitung, d.h. zum Lesen der Aufgabe, zur Bildbetrachtung und ggf. dem Anfertigen von Notizen, gegeben werden. Alle Abbildungen der Speaking-Aufgaben finden Sie zum Ausdrucken (ggf. farbig) und Laminieren auf der beiliegenden CD-ROM.

Aufgaben zur Abfrage von **sprachlichen Mitteln** (Wortschatz und Grammatik) finden Sie im zweiten Teil dieses Hefts. Da zunehmend die kommunikative Gesamtleistung des Schülers im Vordergrund steht, ist diese Art von Aufgabe nicht mehr in allen Bundesländern Bestandteil von Klassenarbeiten. Vielmehr sind sie für den Einsatz in kleineren Tests gedacht.

Sollten Sie bislang mit den *Green Line* 2 Standardaufgaben arbeiten, können Sie die Vorschläge zur Leistungsmessung zusätzlich installieren, um dann auf einen erweiterten Aufgabenpool zugreifen zu können. Mehr dazu erfahren Sie im Handbuch auf der Lehrersoftware.

Wir wünschen Ihnen weiterhin viel Erfolg und Freude bei der Arbeit mit *Green Line!*

Inhalt

Unit 1 Back to school

1 Listening: Back at school

Either:
Mr Barton is a teacher at Thomas Tallis School. He's talking to Tina and Jody.
Listen. What are they talking about? Tick (✔) the right answers.

Italian food	☐	holidays on a farm	☐
surfing	☐	the rain in Cornwall	☐
feeding the animals	☐	holidays with grandma and grandad	☐
swimming	☐	History	☐
abseiling	☐	English	☐
picnic	☐	school clubs	☐

Or:
Mr Barton is a teacher at Thomas Tallis School. He's talking to Tina and Jody.
Read the sentences. Then listen and underline the mistakes (Fehler).

1. Jody, Tina and Mr Barton are talking about after-school clubs.
2. When Jody was in Italy, she ate pizza every day.
3. In the holidays, Tina stayed with her uncle and aunt in Cornwall.
4. In the first few days, Tina went surfing every day.
5. Mr Barton is Jody and Tina's English teacher.

2 Listening: Big trouble

Tina has got a problem. She's talking about it to her mum. *Listen and answer the questions.*

1. What can't Tina find?

   ____

2. She had it in Maths lesson. Say how you know this.

   ____

3. Who has got it now?

   ____

4. Where did she find it?

   ____

5. What must Tina do before her friend comes to visit?

   ____

ISBN: 978-3-12-560016-4

3 Reading: A special day

On Thursday afternoon Sam was late home from school again. It was almost four o'clock when he finally arrived. But Sam was often late, so his mother wasn't worried.

Sam: Hi, Mum.
Mum: Oh, there you are, Sam. You sound very happy today. Did you have a good day at school?
Sam: No, Mum, I didn't have a good day at school. I had a great day!
Mum: Oh? Did you get your English test back?
Sam: No, we didn't have English today. We had a special assembly instead[1].
Mum: A special assembly? Is that why you're late?
Sam: Yes. It was a special assembly for a very special visitor. Guess who!
Mum: I've no idea. Give me a clue[2].

So Sam put his left hand over his right eye. Then with his right hand he picked up a knife[3] from the kitchen table and started to dance.

Mum: A pirate?
Sam: Oh, Mum. Not just a pirate! Captain Jack Sparrow!
Mum: You mean Johnny Depp came to your school today?
Sam: Yes. One of the girls in Mrs Green's tutor group wrote to him last week and asked him for help. She told him that they wanted to mutiny[4] against the teachers. So he came down to help her!
Mum: And Johnny Depp thought that was a good idea?
Sam: Oh yes, Mum. He thought it was a great idea. But of course we didn't mutiny against the teachers. We all sang pirate songs together and Captain Jack Sparrow danced to them! Look, I've got a film of him on my mobile.

[1]instead – *stattdessen*, [2]clue – *hier: Tipp*, [3]knife – *Messer*, [4]to mutiny – *meutern*

Either:
Read the text. Tick (✔) the right answer.

	right	wrong	not in the text
1. On Thursday afternoon Sam was late home again.	✔		
2. It was after 4 o'clock when he got home.			
3. His mum was worried because he was late.			
4. He was happy because they had an interesting English lesson.			
5. Sam's favourite subject is English.			
6. Johnny Depp came to the school because one of the pupils asked him for help.			
7. Johnny Depp sang all the songs from the film Pirates of the Caribbean.			
8. Sam took a photo of Captain Jack Sparrow.			

Or:
Read the text. Answer the questions in complete sentences.

1. On Thursday afternoon Sam was late home from school. Why wasn't his mother worried?
2. Why was Sam late?
3. Why did Johnny Depp come to Sam's school?
4. What did the pupils in Mrs Green's tutor group want to do?
5. What did they do at the special assembly?
6. What does Sam have on his mobile?

Green Line 2
Vorschläge zur Leistungsmessung
ISBN: 978-3-12-560016-4

4 Writing: Last Saturday

Lisa's friend Maria lives in Germany. She is working on the project "Everyday life in Europe" and wants to know more about everyday life in Britain. So last Saturday Lisa took some pictures. *Look at the pictures and write an e-mail to Maria. Use some of these words:* first, then, later, after that, in the afternoon / evening, after breakfast.

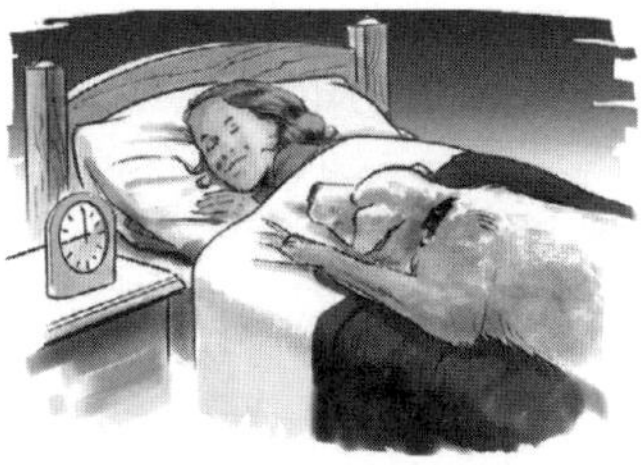

wake up – 9 o'clock

eat – white bread

take – Barker – park

meet friends – town

1 o'clock – have lunch

go – sports club

From:	lisa@funmail.uk	Address book
To:	maria@funmail.de	
Subject:	Your project	

Dear Maria,

Here is some information about my everyday life. I took a few fictures, too.

Last Saturday I

5 Writing: Life and school in the past

It's project week and Sam is working on the project "Life and school in the past". He wants to make a poster and has got three pictures. He must write a short text for the pictures, so people know what they are about. *Choose **one** of the pictures and write a short text. Take notes first.*

1. Marcus's school in 210

2. Anne's life in 1400

3. Jane's school in 1885

Green Line 2
Vorschläge zur Leistungsmessung
ISBN: 978-3-12-560016-4

6 Speaking: Holidays

a) Tina took some pictures in the summer holidays.
Now she is showing and explaining them to her friend.

b) *Bring some of your holiday pictures to school. Talk about what you did in the holidays.*

7 Speaking: School

A: You're visiting a school in Britain. The pupils there ask you to talk about school in Germany.
Look at the pictures for help.
You can start like this: In Germany pupils don't wear …

B: You're from Great Britain. You're visiting a school in Germany. The pupils there ask you to talk about school in Britain.
Look at the pictures for help.
You can start like this: Pupils in Britain must wear …

School rules

→ Don't play football in the corridor.
→ Don't use your mobile phone in lessons.

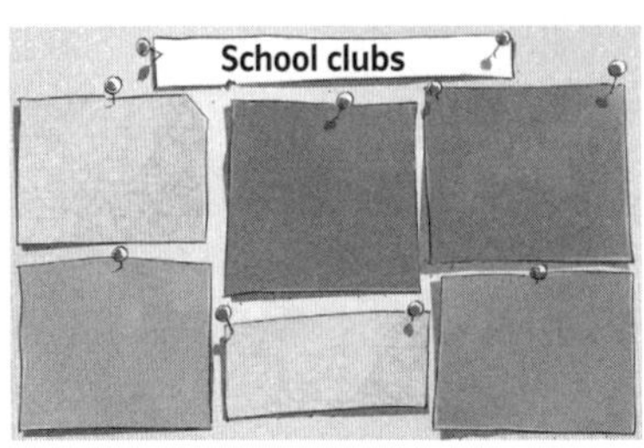

Green Line 2
Vorschläge zur Leistungsmessung
ISBN: 978-3-12-560016-4

8 Mediation: At a party

You meet an English boy at a party. He doesn't speak very much German.
So you talk to him in English.

1. Du stellst dich vor und fragst ihn, wie er heißt.

   You: ______________________________

   Tom: Hi. My name is Tom.

2. Nun willst du wissen, woher er kommt.

   You: ______________________________

   Tom: I'm from Newquay. That's in Cornwall.

3. Du erzählst ihm, dass du Newquay kennst, weil ihr in den Sommerferien zwei Wochen dort verbracht habt.

   You: ______________________________

   ____

   Tom: Oh, that's nice. Did you have a good time?

4. Du bejahst und sagst, dass Newquay toll war.

   You: ______________________________

   Tom: So what did you do there? Did you go surfing?

5. Du verneinst, sagst ihm aber, dass ihr jeden Tag im Meer geschwommen seid.

   You: ______________________________

   ____

   Tom: Where did you stay? Were you at a campsite or in a hotel?

6. Ihr wart auf einem Campingplatz in der Nähe vom Strand.

   You: ______________________________

   Tom: Oh yes. I know the campsite. It's near my best friend's house. Was it good?

7. Du bejahst und sagst, dass du viele nette Menschen dort kennen gelernt hast.

   You: ______________________________

   Tom: Oh, good.

8. Du sagst, dass du hoffst, dass er eine gute Zeit in Deutschland hat.

   You: ______________________________

ISBN: 978-3-12-560016-4

Unit 2 Welcome to London

1 Listening: A day out in London

Jody spent the day in London. Now she's telling her mum all about it.
Listen. Tick (✔) the right answer.

	right	wrong
1. Jody and Tina met James and Betty on their way into London.	✔	
2. They met them on the Tube.		
3. Betty is James's cousin and doesn't live in Greenwich.		
4. James and Betty were on their way to the zoo.		
5. They wanted to see the new baby elephant there.		
6. There are usually a lot of people at the zoo on Saturdays.		
7. James and Betty were lucky. They didn't wait long in the queue.		
8. The four teenagers had lunch together in Oxford Street.		
9. After lunch Betty and James went to Harrods.		
10. On their way home, Jody and Tina saw Ben and Nasreen.		

2 Listening: A trip to London

Betty has been to London. Now she is back at home and she's visiting her best friend, Anna Cook.
Listen to the text and finish the sentences.

1. When Betty arrived at the Cooks' house, Anna didn't hear Betty because she was ______________

____

2. While she was in London, Betty stayed ______________________________
3. They have got ______________________________ in Greenwich.
4. Betty didn't see all of the sights because ______________________________

____

5. While she was in London, she bought ______________________________
6. Anna likes it very much. She says ______________________________

Green Line 2
Vorschläge zur Leistungsmessung
ISBN: 978-3-12-560016-4

3 Reading: A trip to the theatre

Last Saturday Terry and his mum went to the Theatre Royal in Covent Garden. They had tickets for a musical there. Mr Jackson didn't go with them because he was busy. The show started at half past two, so Terry and his mum left the house at quarter to twelve. They travelled from Greenwich to Bank Station by DLR. Then they changed onto the Tube. First they took the Central Line to Holborn and after that the Piccadilly Line southbound to Covent Garden.

At quarter past two, they arrived at the theatre. There was a long queue at the door, but they already had tickets so they didn't need to wait. Five minutes later, they were sitting in their seats[1] in Row[2] 4. The seats next to them were still empty, but there was a young man in the seat at the end of the row. He looked very funny. He was wearing a big grey cape[3] and a grey hat[4] with three corners. While Terry was looking at the man, two women arrived and sat down in the seats next to him. When Terry looked again, the man in the funny clothes was no longer there.

After the show, Terry's dad met them outside the theatre and drove them home in his taxi. When Terry told him about the man in the funny grey clothes, Mr Jackson was very excited.
"Were you in Row 4?", he asked. "Yes, we were", answered Terry. "Why?" – "Because that is where 'The Man in Grey' always sits", said Mr Jackson. "And who's he?", Terry wanted to know. "Oh, Terry! Don't you know 'The Man in Grey'?" asked Dad. "He's London's most famous theatre ghost[5]!"

[1]seat – *Sitz, Platz*; [2]row – *Reihe*; [3]cape – *Umhang*; [4]hat – *Hut*; [5]ghost – *Gespenst*

Either:
Read the text. Put the sentences into the right order.

______ When they arrived at the theatre, they sat down in Row 4.

______ Later Mr Jackson told Terry that the man was London's most famous theatre ghost.

______ A moment later, the man was no longer there.

___1___ Last Saturday Terry and his mother went to the theatre together.

______ At the end of the row, Terry saw a young man.

______ They travelled to Covent Garden by DLR and by Tube.

______ Mr Jackson didn't go with them because he didn't have time.

______ He was wearing funny grey clothes.

Or:
Read the text. Answer the questions in complete sentences.

1. When did Terry and his mother go the theatre?
2. Why didn't Mr Jackson go with them?
3. How did they get there?
4. When they arrived, there was a long queue. Why didn't they need to wait?
5. Where did they sit?
6. A young man was sitting at the end of the row. What was he wearing?
7. Who is 'The Man in Grey'?
8. Why do people call him 'The Man in Grey'?

Green Line 2
Vorschläge zur Leistungsmessung
ISBN: 978-3-12-560016-4

4 Writing: A day in London

On your last birthday you got a special present from your parents – a day in London.
On the next day you write in your travel diary:

- where you went first (Buckingham Palace, the London Eye, Greenwich, …).
- how you got there (bus, Tube, river boat, walk).
- why you liked / didn't like it (boring, interesting, exciting, fun, …).
- where you had lunch (café, restaurant, park, …).
- what you did after lunch (ice skating, shopping, …).
- what you did in the evening (theatre, cinema, …).

Start like this: For my birthday I got a very special present from my parents – a day in London. When we got to London, we first …

5 Writing: A photo story

Ben and Nasreen are still best friends. To remind (erinnern) them of how it first started, Lisa and Rob made a little photo story.
Look at the pictures and write complete sentences. Use the past tense (simple and progressive).

first – go – Covent Garden

while – listen to – phone

after that – give map – leave

while – open map – note – fall out

note from Nasreen – want to meet – London Eye – 10.30

try to phone – mobile not on

so – catch next bus – London Eye

there – see – hold hands – kiss

later – follow – Waterloo Station

train – arrive – get on

but then – doors close – leave without

Start like this:

On Saturday Lisa, Ben and Rob wanted to do a sightseeing tour of London. First they went to Covent Garden. While they …

Green Line 2
Vorschläge zur Leistungsmessung
ISBN: 978-3-12-560016-4

6 Speaking: London

*Work in pairs or groups of three. Choose **one** of the tasks.*

a) There are a lot of things to see and do in London, but you've only got two days there. *Discuss what you want to do on the first and second day. Come to an agreement.*
b) You are in London and it's a nice day. *Discuss what you want to do.*
c) You are in London and it's raining. *Discuss what you want to do.*
d) It's your last day in London and each of you has only got £5 left for sightseeing. *Discuss what you want to do.*

Madame Tussauds

Madame Tussauds came to London in 1803 and showed 30 wax figures in Baker St, in a house near to today's museum. If you like the idea of wax film and sport stars and figures of the Royal Family, then Madame Tussauds is a 'must'. You can take a ride in the Spirit of London 'time taxi', too, where you sit in a black taxi and drive through London's history in five minutes.

- Underground: Baker St
- adult / child £24 / £20
- 09:30 – 17:30 Mon – Fri, 09:00 – 18:00 Sat & Sun

Tower of London

The Tower of London is a real 'must', when you are in London. The castle on the River Thames is almost a thousand years old. In the past many people were killed here. But kings and queens lived here, too.

- Underground: Tower Hill
- adult / child / family £16 / £9.50 / £45
- 09:00 – 18:00 Tue – Sat, Mar – Oct
  10:00 – 18:00 Sun & Mon, Mar – Oct
  09:00 – 17:00 Tue – Sat, Nov – Feb
  10:00 – 17:00 Sun & Mon, Nov – Feb

Buckingham Palace

In 1837 the Royal Family first moved into this palace. The Royals still use it today. You can tell when the Queen is at home – the flag is on top of the building.
Visitors can see 19 of the 661 rooms in August and September when the Queen is on holiday in Scotland.

- Underground: St James's Park, Victoria, Green Park
- adult / child / family £15 / £8.50 / £38.50
- 09:30 – 16:30 28 Jul – 25 Sep

Westminster

Parliament is here, in the Palace of Westminster. Charles Barry built it between 1840 and 1860. When Parliament meets, visitors can listen to the discussions there. The Clock Tower, known as Big Ben, outside the building is very famous. Once every five years cleaners abseil and wash the clock's hands and face.

- Underground: Westminster
- when Parliament meets: 14:30 – 22:30 Mon, 11:30 – 19:00 Tue & Wed, 11:30 – 18:30 Thu, 09:30 – 15:00 Fri

Hyde Park

With its beautiful gardens and grass, Hyde Park is London's most famous and largest Royal Park. It was the first royal park to open to the public about 400 years ago.
In the summer people throw Frisbees there, or sit on the grass and enjoy the sun or have a picnic. It's a great place for open-air concerts, too. Every morning soldiers ride through the park on their way to Horse Guards Parade in Whitehall.

- Underground: Knightsbridge, Hyde Park Corner, Lancaster Gate, Marble Arch
- 05:30 – 24:00

Green Line 2
Vorschläge zur Leistungsmessung
ISBN: 978-3-12-560016-4

7 Mediation: A visit to the Natural History Museum

Your family wants to spend the Christmas holidays in London. While you're there, you want to see the dinosaurs (Dinosaurier), the blue whale (Blauwal) and the giant squid (Riesentintenfisch) in the Natural History Museum. You find this information on the Internet:

The Natural History Museum

Visit our fascinating dinosaurs, blue whale and giant squid at the Natural History Museum, and see much more. It's great fun for the whole family.

How to contact us:	
Address:	Cromwell Road, London SW7 5BD
Telephone:	+44 (0)20 7942 5000
Web:	www.nhm.ac.uk
Tickets:	free
Opening times:	
Open every day:	10:00 - 17:50 Mon - Sat, 11:00 - 17:50 Sun
Closed:	24 - 26 December
How to get here:	
By Tube:	We are just a short walk from South Kensington Station on the District, Circle and Piccadilly lines
By bus:	Bus numbers 14, 49, 70, 74, 345, 360, 414 and C1 all stop near here.

Answer your parents' questions in German.

1. Was gibt es dort zu sehen? (Schreibe Stichpunkte)

___

2. Was kostet der Eintritt?

___

3. Hat das Museum jeden Tag auf?

___

4. Wo genau ist das Museum?

___

5. Wie kommt man am besten dorthin?

___

Green Line 2
Vorschläge zur Leistungsmessung
ISBN: 978-3-12-560016-4

Unit 3 Pocket money

1 Listening: Shopping at the supermarket

Tina and her mum want to go food shopping. *Listen and answer the questions. (Take notes.)*

1. Where is the shopping list? ______________________
2. Why didn't Tina tell her mum about the list she saw? ______________________
3. How many things does Mrs Cole want to buy? ______________________
4. When will the guests[1] come? ______________________
5. What do Mrs Cole and Tina want to buy?

☐ bacon	☐ ice-cream	☐ drinks
☐ hamburgers	☐ chips	☐ salad
☐ fresh vegetables	☐ chocolate cakes	☐ pizza
☐ fruit	☐ bread	☐ meat

6. What time is it when the two want to pay? ______________________
7. How much is the shopping? ______________________
8. Where is Mrs Cole's money? ______________________

[1]guest – *Gast*

2 Listening: Pocket money ideas

Either:
Tina, Jody and James are in town. *Listen. In which order are they going to do these things? Write down the numbers 1 to 4.*

Or:
Tina, Jody and James are in town. *Listen. Are the sentences right or wrong? Tick (✔) the right answers. Then correct the wrong sentences.*

	right	wrong
1. James is going to go to the cinema with his friends in the evening.		
2. They all want to meet on Saturday to watch a DVD together.		
3. They all want to eat something first.		
4. James has got other ideas for his pocket money.		
5. James likes funny clothes, too.		
6. James wants to buy a new DVD.		

Green Line 2
Vorschläge zur Leistungsmessung
ISBN: 978-3-12-560016-4

3 Reading: That's how we spend our pocket money

Jill, 13 – "I don't get much pocket money, but my sister, brother and I all do different jobs at home and we get some money for it. We get money for cleaning[1] our rooms – £1.50, £1 for cleaning the kitchen and £2 for cleaning the bathroom. That's great. I get some money, too, when I go shopping for my mum: she always gives me £2. I like it because then I can buy a magazine. But I save money for nice clothes, too."

Julie, 12 – "I get pocket money and I save it! I want to visit my friend in Germany next year and I need a lot of money for that. I like nice clothes, pizza and my mobile, but everything is very expensive. Sometimes I change clothes with a friend, it's cheaper than buying new clothes and we have a lot of fun. I never eat at the school cafeteria. I make my sandwiches at home so I can save money. Sometimes I help my mum at home and I get money for that."

Tracy, 12 – "I get pocket money – £5 a week. I usually save the money because I want to buy new CDs and top-up cards for my mobile. That's expensive! I haven't got a job because I have a lot of homework. When grandad and grandma come to visit us, they often give me extra pocket money. This is great and helps me because I can buy some great things."

[1]to clean – *säubern, reinigen*

Either:

Read what Jill, Julie and Tracy say. Tick (✔) the right answer(s).

1. She has got a sister and a brother. ☐ Jill ☐ Julie ☐ Tracy
2. She gets pocket money from her grandma and grandad. ☐ Jill ☐ Julie ☐ Tracy
3. She wants to visit her German friend next year. ☐ Jill ☐ Julie ☐ Tracy
4. She sometimes helps her mum at home. ☐ Jill ☐ Julie ☐ Tracy
5. She changes her clothes with her friends. ☐ Jill ☐ Julie ☐ Tracy

Or:

Match the beginnings and the endings.

1. Jill, Tracy and Julie	a) because they are three children at home.
2. Jill likes	b) magazines.
3. Jill and Julie help at home because	c) she goes shopping for her.
4. Jill doesn't get a lot of pocket money	d) save some money.
5. Julie saves some money because	e) she uses her pocket money.
6. Julie has got good friends because	f) they change clothes.
7. When Tracy wants to buy a top-up card,	g) she never eats at school.
8. Jill gets money from her mum because	h) they get money for it.

1. ______ 2. ______ 3. ______ 4. ______ 5. ______ 6. ______ 7. ______ 8. ______

Green Line 2
Vorschläge zur Leistungsmessung
ISBN: 978-3-12-560016-4

4 Writing: More pocket money

You would like to have some more pocket money. Your parents ask you to write down how much money you'd like to have, what you'd like to spend the money on, and what jobs around the house you'd be ready to do. *Write about 80 words.*

5 Writing: Talk to a shop assistant

You go into a shop because you want to buy a new mobile phone.
Write a dialogue. These ideas can help you:

you:

- say hello
- say what you are looking for
- ask about the price
- talk about the colour
- ask for another mobile
- say that it is OK
- ask for a £5 top-up card
- say goodbye

shop assistant:

- say hello
- ask if the customer needs help
- inform about the price
- show another mobile phone
- bring a top-up card
- say where the customer can pay
- say goodbye

Green Line 2
Vorschläge zur Leistungsmessung
ISBN: 978-3-12-560016-4

6 Speaking: Money

You got 50 euros for your birthday. Say what you are going to do with the money.
What are / aren't you going to spend the money on? Why? Here are some ideas:

?

7 Speaking: Pocket money

How are you going to persuade (überzeugen) your parents to give you more money?
Work in pairs. One of you takes the role of a teenager and asks his / her mum / dad for more pocket money. The other one takes the role of the parent. Before you start, think of some good arguments (Argumente).

teenager	parent
• buy clothes on my own • friends get more money • …	• think he / she gets a lot • do jobs around the house • …

8 Mediation: A role-play

A	B
Du arbeitest in einem Fastfood-Restaurant als Bedienung.	*Du bist in einem Fastfood-Restaurant und möchtest etwas zu essen bestellen.*
	Sage, dass du einen LargeMc und Pommes dazu haben möchtest.
Frage, welche Größe die Pommesportion haben soll: klein, mittel oder groß, und ob B Ketchup möchte.	
	Sage, dass du eine mittlere Portion mit Ketchup möchtest.
Frage, ob B auch etwas zu trinken haben möchte.	
	Lehne dankend ab.
Sage, dass es £3,78 macht.	
	Du gibst der Verkäuferin £5.
Bedanke dich und gib £1,22 Rückgeld.	
	Bedanke und verabschiede dich.

Green Line 2
Vorschläge zur Leistungsmessung
ISBN: 978-3-12-560016-4

9 Mediation: Shopping for new clothes

Cornelia is visiting her friend Sheila in London. Cornelia needs a new T-shirt and a pair of jeans. Sheila helps her friend from Germany in the shop.
Write down what Sheila is saying.

Cornelia: Bitte sage der Verkäuferin, dass ich ein neues T-Shirt und eine neue Jeans brauche.

Sheila: Excuse me, please. My friend ______________________________

____

Assistant: What sizes does she need? What T-shirt colour does she want?

Sheila: ______________________________

____

Cornelia: Ich glaube, für die Jeans Größe M und für das T-Shirt S. Ich suche ein rotes T-Shirt.

Sheila: ______________________________

____

Assistant: Here is the pair of jeans in size M and the T-shirt in size S. Does she like the colour? She can try them on.

Sheila: ______________________________

____

Cornelia: Ja, das Rot gefällt mir. Wo sind denn hier die Umkleidekabinen?

Sheila: ______________________________

____

Assistant: They are just around the corner.

Sheila: ______________________________

____

Cornelia: Die Jeans sind zu teuer. Ich nehme nur das T-Shirt. Frag bitte, wo wir zahlen sollen.

Sheila: ______________________________

____

Assistant: It's OK. You can pay over there.

Sheila: ______________________________

____

Green Line 2
Vorschläge zur Leistungsmessung
ISBN: 978-3-12-560016-4

Unit 4 Who wants to be a star?

1 Listening: Robbie Williams

Either:

Robbie Williams is ill. So his manager does the interview for him.
Listen. Are the sentences right or wrong? Tick (✔) the right answer.

	right	wrong
1. Robbie was born in Shenstone, Staffordshire.		
2. He lived with his mum and his dad.		
3. His father liked to perform songs and tricks.		
4. He was good at school.		
5. He told a lot of jokes at school.		
6. He liked performing and singing and always wanted to become famous.		
7. He saw that they were looking for boys between 16 and 17 on a poster.		
8. The audition was the beginning of *Take That*.		
9. Robbie Williams left the band because he had problems singing the songs the others wanted to sing.		
10. The band is back because they need money.		

Or:

Robbie Williams is ill. So his manager does the interview for him.
Listen and answer the questions. (Take notes.)

1. Where was Robbie Williams born?
2. Who did Robbie live with?
3. What was his father's job?
4. What do you get to know about his life before *Take That*?
5. Where did he meet the other boys?
6. Why did Robbie leave the band in 1995?
7. When was the end of *Take That*?
8. When did *Take That* get together again?

2 Listening: Stars and their prizes

Listen to what the stars are saying. Tick (✔) the right answer and fill in the missing information.

	won a prize yet?	plans to win another prize?	if not, why?
football player	yes ☐ no ☐	yes ☐ no ☐	
singer	yes ☐ no ☐	yes ☐ no ☐	
actor	yes ☐ no ☐	yes ☐ no ☐	
model	yes ☐ no ☐	yes ☐ no ☐	

Green Line 2
Vorschläge zur Leistungsmessung
ISBN: 978-3-12-560016-4

3 Reading: Britain's Got Talent

Britain's Got Talent (BGT) is a British TV show[1] and part of the Got Talent[2] series[3]. You can see a lot of singers, dancers and other interesting people on this show. They all take part in the competition and audition for a jury[4], people in the studio[5] and at home in front of the TV. The winner gets £ 100,000 and can later perform at the *Royal Variety Performance* in front of the Royal Family.
Simon Cowell started the series of talent shows in 2007. For every series about 200 people come and perform in front of a jury in towns like Manchester, Glasgow, Birmingham, Cardiff and London. Usually there are three people in the jury. If the judges don't like an act[6], they push a buzzer[7] which then shows a large red X on the stage. If all three judges push their buzzers, the act must end. The best 40 acts make it to the semi-finals[8], and the most popular acts from the semi-finals get through to the final. After the last act people can call in for the act they liked the best. The act with the highest number of calls wins the show.
Paul Potts, theatre singer and shop-assistant in a mobile phone shop, won the first series and became famous. After the show almost 700,000 people bought his CD. In 2008 street-dancer George Sampson went on to win the second series and the dance group *Diversity* won the third series. In June 2010 the acrobatic gymnastics[9] group *Spelbound* won first prize.
Some people didn't like the series because they felt that it had become more important for TV to show people who were not good at something, and not people with real talent. And those who took part in the auditions said they didn't get any food or anything to drink while they were waiting to get on stage – and some of them waited for 10 hours.

[1]show – *Sendung*; [2]talent – *Talent*; [3]series – *Serie*, Folge; [4]jury – *Jury*; [5]studio – *(Fernseh-)Studio*; [6]act – *Darbietung*; [7]buzzer – *Knopf, Hupe*; [8]semi-final – *Halbfinale*; [9]acrobatic gymnastics – *Akrobaten*

Either:
Read the text and tick (✔) the right answer(s).

1. People that like to … take part in the show.
   - ☐ sing
   - ☐ dance
   - ☐ do sports

2. You can watch the show …
   - ☐ at home.
   - ☐ on the Internet.
   - ☐ in the studio.

3. The winner …
   - ☐ gets some money.
   - ☐ can show his / her skills in front of the Royal Family.
   - ☐ wins tickets for a Royal Variety Performance show.

4. Auditions take place …
   - ☐ in a theatre.
   - ☐ in front of the Royal Family.
   - ☐ in different British cities.

5. … the winner of the final.
   - ☐ People in the studio choose
   - ☐ The jury chooses
   - ☐ People that phone from home choose

6. The good thing is that …
   - ☐ people with little talent can win some money to practise their skills.
   - ☐ normal people with talent can become famous.
   - ☐ people with little talent can meet the Royal Family.

Or:
Read the text. What's good and not so good about the show?

good	not so good

Green Line 2
Vorschläge zur Leistungsmessung
ISBN: 978-3-12-560016-4

4 Writing: My favourite ...

Your friend has written you an e-mail. *Read the e-mail and answer it.*
Write six to eight sentences about your favourite star.

Hi,
Guess what! Last night Lady Gaga was on TV again. At the moment she's my favourite star. I like her crazy songs. Did you know that nobody knew her before she started to write her songs? She has made a lot of money with her songs and she has got a lot of fans. I've got all her CDs but I've never been to a concert. I like her clothes most. They are funny. I've never seen anybody like her and I'd like to be a star like her, too. Who is your favourite star?
Write soon. R.

From:	me@funmail.uk	Address book
To:	you@funmail.com	
Subject:	Stars	

____

____

____

____

____

____

____

5 Writing: An audition

There's an audition next week and you want to take part in it.
Write to your friend and say what you have/haven't done for the audition.

Hi _______________

____

____

____

____

____

____

____

____

Think about ...

- how you found out about the audition.
- the song you'd like to perform
- dancing
- clothes
- hair
- why you want to go there
- ...

Green Line 2
Vorschläge zur Leistungsmessung
ISBN: 978-3-12-560016-4

6 Speaking: Would you like to be a star?

Would you like to be a star? *Work in pairs. Say what is good or not so good about it.*
You can start like this:
A: I think it's nice to be a star because you can …
B: You're right. But …

?

7 Mediation: Stars

Work in pairs and do an interview with a star.

Interviewer	Star
Begrüße deinen Gast.	
	Sage, dass du dich freust, da zu sein.
Sage, dass du auf seinem Konzert warst und es toll fandest. Frage, ob S vor seinen Auftritten nervös ist.	
	Sage, dass du manchmal nervös bist, wenn du vor vielen Leuten spielst.
Frage, ob S etwas Besonderes macht bevor er / sie auf die Bühne geht.	
	Sage, dass du dir vorher immer einen Penny in die Hosentasche steckst.
Sage, dass du das interessant findest. Frage, wie alles angefangen hat.	
	Sage, dass du einige deiner Songs ins Internet gestellt hast.
Frage, ob S es schön findet, nun – 5 Jahre später – berühmt zu sein.	
	Sage, dass du es toll findest. Allerdings bleibt nicht viel Zeit für Freunde und Familie. Du bist oft nicht zu Hause. Außerdem bist du oft im Fernsehen und gibst Interviews. Da ist es schwer, Zeit für neue Songs zu finden, sie zu schreiben und zu proben. Aber du wolltest schon als Kind Popstar werden.
Bedanke dich für das Gespräch und wünsche S weiterhin viel Glück.	
	Bedanke und verabschiede dich.

ISBN: 978-3-12-560016-4

8 Mediation: Teen Buzz Magazine

Your friend from England brought the Teen Buzz magazine with him / her. Your mum sees you looking at this page again and again. *Read the page. Answer you mum's questions in German.*

TEEN BUZZ MAGAZINE NEEDS YOU!

You are between 10 and 16 years old and want to be part of our music show this summer in Greenwich?

We are looking for singers that like to be on stage. If you think you have what it takes, come to our audition.

When: Monday, 3 March from 5 – 8 pm

Where: Greenwich Youth Club, 11 Firle Road, Greenwich

What to bring: Yourself, a good voice, clothes that show your personal style, and some of your fans

We will have a live band for your music and special lights for the show in August. We will help you with your clothes, hair and make-up, too. The winner will meet his / her favourite star and record his / her song.

Interested? For more information write to: **sheilah@castingpeople.com**

[1]to record – *aufnehmen*

Mutter: Was liest du da?

Du: ______________________________

Mutter: Wer veranstaltet das Casting?

Du: ______________________________

Mutter: Wann findet das Casting statt?

Du: ______________________________

Mutter: Was musst du dafür können und mitbringen?

Du: ______________________________

Mutter: Wow, das klingt gut. Und wo ist dieses Casting?

Du: ______________________________

Mutter: Für was für eine Show ist das Casting?

Du: ______________________________

Mutter: Und was kann man da gewinnen?

Du: ______________________________

Green Line 2
Vorschläge zur Leistungsmessung
ISBN: 978-3-12-560016-4

Unit 5 Fit for life

1 Listening: Is it the same everywhere?

Either:
Yannik is German. He is visiting a friend in England.

a) *Listen to Yannik and James. Use the boxes and mark the sports Yannik talks about with 'Y' and the sports James talks about with 'J'.*

 ☐ ______
 ☐ ______
 ☐ ______
 ☐ ______

 ☐ ______
 ☐ ______
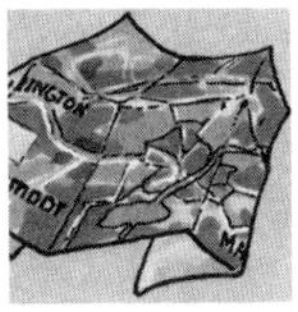 ☐ ______
 ☐ ______

b) *Which sports do they do regularly? Write down the name under the picture.*

Or:
Yannik is German. He is visiting a friend in England. *Answer the questions in 1 to 5 words.*

1. What does James never have for breakfast? ______
2. When is James going to go to orienteering club? ______
3. Name two things you need to go orienteering. ______
4. To win orienteering you need to … ______
5. Where does Yannik do sports? ______
6. What's the same in England and Germany? ______

2 Listening: At the hospital

a) *Tina is talking to a doctor. Listen and tick (✔) the parts of her body which hurt.*

b) This is Tina's sick note (Entschuldigung) to school.
Complete the sentences with the right words.

Tina can't come to school today because she broke her ______ yesterday when she was playing ______. She hasn't got a ______ but she feels ______, so she must stay at home today. She hurt her big toe, too, while she was going into the ______. A man was walking quickly and he ______ on to her foot. This week Tina cannot write the ______.

Green Line 2
Vorschläge zur Leistungsmessung
ISBN: 978-3-12-560016-4

3 Reading: Young sportsperson of the year

Nick Edwards has just been chosen young sportsperson of the year. Our reporter spoke to him yesterday at his home near Nottingham.

Reporter: Nick, you're only 16 and you're already one of the best horseback riders[1] in Britain. I'd like to ask you how it all started. When did you first ride a horse?

Nick: When I was about seven. My big sister loved horses and wanted to learn to ride. My mum took her for lessons and I went, too, because I couldn't stay at home alone. After some time I started to enjoy it and the trainer, Tod, said that I did everything very well. He taught me everything he knew. He's a great trainer.

Reporter: Who else[2] helped you learn to ride so well?

Nick: My sister. She taught me to understand horses. And she still helps me to keep fit.

Reporter: Is that very important for horseback riding?

Nick: Yes, it is. You need to be strong and you mustn't become overweight. I always eat healthily and I do lots of other sports. I have a fitness plan because it's hard for me to keep fit.

Reporter: Who writes your fitness plan?

Nick: My trainer and my mother write it together. My mother says that she must cook the food so she helps me, too. She says that I need time to meet friends and just chill[3].

Reporter: And do you have enough time to meet your friends? Tell me about your day.

Nick: I get up early and feed the horses. Then I jog for thirty minutes – usually with my sister – before I have breakfast. After breakfast I ride my favourite horse, Robin Good, if he's fit, and we usually jump. My trainer plans the training sessions[4]. So I have two plans – a fitness and a training plan. In the afternoon I go riding again or I go swimming. In the evening I've got lots of time to meet my friends. But I mustn't go to bed late because I always get up early in the morning.

Reporter: Thank you very much for the interview.

[1]horseback rider – *Reiter/-in;* [2]else – *sonst noch;* [3]to chill – *relaxen, sich entspannen;* [4]session – *Einheit*

a) *Read the article. Are the sentences right or wrong?*

	right	wrong
1. Nick is the best horseback rider in Britain.		
2. Nick's trainer and sister helped him learn to ride.		
3. Horseback riders must be very fit.		
4. Nick's plans tell him what he should eat and how he should keep fit.		
5. Nick's mum thinks he spends too much time with his friends.		
6. Nick does sport in the morning and in the afternoon.		

b) *Correct the wrong sentences from* a).

____

____

____

Green Line 2
Vorschläge zur Leistungsmessung
ISBN: 978-3-12-560016-4

4 Writing: An accident

You saw how an accident happened.
Look at the pictures and notes and write a report about it. Use the past tense.

ride his bike

kick the ball

can't stop

take him to hospital

On Saturday at about 11 o'clock ______________________________

____

____

____

____

____

____

5 Writing: Family pictures

In an interview Molly talks about her career (Karriere). She shows the reporters some of her pictures, too. *Use the pictures and write an article about Molly.*

Molly is in Year 10 but she is already one of the best women tennis players in Britain. In an interview she told us about how it all started and how she keeps fit.

____

____

____

____

____

____

Green Line 2
Vorschläge zur Leistungsmessung
ISBN: 978-3-12-560016-4

6 Speaking: How do you keep fit?

a) *Look at the charts (Diagramme). Say what teenagers in Britain do / don't do to keep fit.*

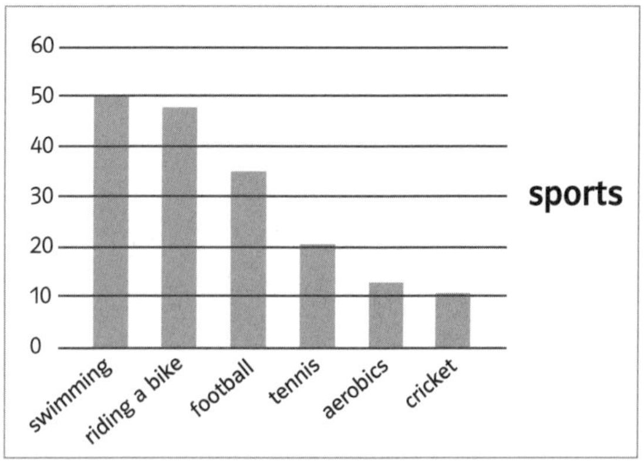

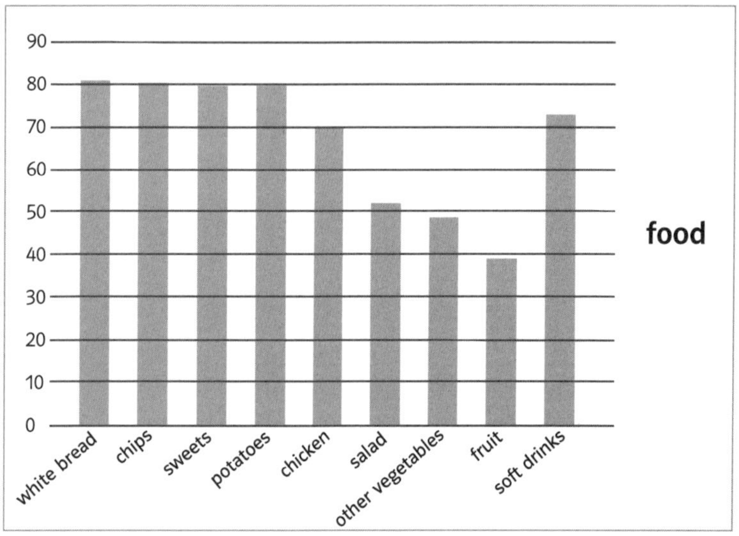

b) *Say what you do to keep fit and stay healthy. These questions and the ideas in* a) *may help you.*

1. Do you eat breakfast every day?
2. Do you smoke?
3. Do you do sports regularly?
4. Does your family do healthy activities together, for example swimming or go for walks?
5. Do you eat fruit and vegetables regularly?
6. How many hours of sleep do you get at night?
7. Do you brush your teeth and wash yourself regularly?
8. Do you go to a sports club in your free-time?
9. Do you go to the doctor regularly?

cricket ['krɪkɪt] *in englischsprachigen Ländern beliebte Ball- und Mannschaftssportart;* potato [pə'teɪtəʊ] – *Kartoffel;* soft drink [sɒft drɪŋk] – *alkoholfreies Getränk wie Cola, Limonade;* to brush [brʌʃ] – *putzen*

7 Speaking: £150 to spend

Your class came first in a competition and won £150.
Work in pairs and discuss (diskutiert) what you want to do with the money.

?

Green Line 2
Vorschläge zur Leistungsmessung
ISBN: 978-3-12-560016-4

8 Mediation: A holiday in the Black Forest

You are visiting a friend in England. Next year he wants to visit you in Germany and see the Black Forest. You look for information on the Internet. *Answer your friend's questions in English.*

Schwarzwald Abenteuerurlaub

Magst du Abenteuer? Magst du Sport? Dann komm mit in den Schwarzwald.

Hier kannst du zwischen vielen Sportarten und Aktivitäten wählen. Du kannst klettern, reiten, Kanufahren, im See schwimmen und natürlich auch spazieren gehen.

Das hast du noch nie gemacht?
Kein Problem. Wir haben großartige Lehrer für jede Sportart. Du wirst überrascht sein, was du am Ende einer Woche schon alles kannst.

Ist es gefährlich?
Klettern und Kanufahren können gefährlich sein, aber nicht wenn man die richtige Ausrüstung hat. Bringt feste Schuhe, warme Sachen und euren Anorak mit. Unsere erfahrenen Lehrer zeigen und erklären euch alles. Aber trotzdem müsst ihr vorsichtig sein.

Unterkunft
Die Unterbringung erfolgt für alle Teilnehmer in einem großen Haus im Herzen des Schwarzwalds. Es gibt sechs große Schlafzimmer mit jeweils zehn Betten.

Kevin: I'm sorry. I can't understand everything. What sports can you do there?

You: ______________________________

____

Kevin: That sounds great, but I've never been in a canoe or on a horse. Who does the teaching?

You: ______________________________

Kevin: Isn't it dangerous[1]? My parents worry when I ride my bike.

You: ______________________________

____

Kevin: Do you need special clothes?

You: ______________________________

Kevin: Where do you stay?

You: ______________________________

____

[1]dangerous – *gefährlich*

ISBN: 978-3-12-560016-4

Unit 6 In Scotland

1 Listening: A weekend in Scotland

Either:

The Cabral family spent a long weekend in Scotland. *Listen to what Jody tells her friends about the weekend, and tick (✔) the right answers.*

	right	wrong
1. Jody and Aaron went to Scotland with their mum and their dog Bruno.		
2. They visited their mum's friends.		
3. It was easy for Bruno to climb to the mountain top.		
4. While they were in Scotland, they climbed Ben Nevis, saw Loch Less and visited Glasgow.		
5. The Cabral family likes picnics.		
6. Jody's brother can't play football on Saturday because he fell and hurt his arm.		
7. Inverness played a football match against Glasgow.		
8. They didn't see Nessie because either[1] the monster doesn't like tourists, or because there is no monster in the lake.		

[1]either – *entweder*

Or:

Tina, Jody and James are talking about the weekend. *Listen and take notes.*

1. Who went to Scotland? ______________________
2. Why did they go to Scotland? ______________________
3. What did they do while they were there? (four things) ______________________

   ____
4. Why is James worried about Aaron? ______________________

   ____
5. Why didn't they see Nessie? ______________________

2 Listening: Weekend plans

It is Friday after school. *Listen and take notes. What are their plans for the weekend?*

Tina: ______________________

____

Jody: ______________________

____

Aaron: ______________________

____

Green Line 2
Vorschläge zur Leistungsmessung
ISBN: 978-3-12-560016-4

3 Reading: The Battle of Bannockburn

Rob is visiting his uncle Bruce in Scotland. Rob is very interested in his uncle's work on the oil platform, but most of all, he likes his stories about Scottish history. Uncle Bruce knows a lot about the kings of Scotland and about their battles. One evening he tells Rob the story of the Battle of Bannockburn, fought by King Robert the Bruce.

"King Robert the Bruce had been hiding in the cave for a while. He watched the spider build its web again and again. Then Robert the Bruce thought that it was time to do something and that he couldn't hide any longer. So he thought that he just needed to be brave[1] enough to win against the English. He told his army that they would go and fight the English army at Bannockburn near Stirling Castle now. When they arrived, the English army didn't think that the Scottish army would be a problem for them. But the Commander[2] of Stirling Castle had an idea of what was about to happen and tried to talk to the English King. He told him they needn't fight against the Scottish army because the English were near to the castle. So the head of the English army could just go and talk to Robert the Bruce."

"And what did the English King do, uncle Bruce? Did he talk to Robert the Bruce?"

"No, Rob, the English King didn't want to talk to Robert the Bruce about Scotland. He told his Earls[3] of Gloucester and Hereford to lead[4] the army against Robert the Bruce. But the earls weren't friends. The Earl of Gloucester wanted to lead the army alone, and so did the Earl of Hereford. So they didn't meet to talk about how they could fight against the Scottish army together." "Oh no, so Gloucester did something else than Hereford? But you can't win a battle if you don't work together!"

"You're right, Rob! Before the battle started there was an English soldier that tried to kill the Scottish King because he saw that Robert the Bruce was alone on his horse. He rode up to him and tried to kill Robert with his sword[5]. But Robert the Bruce was faster than the soldier and killed him with his axe[6]."

"And what happened then?"

"The English army wasn't fast enough. The Scottish army was much faster and the way they fought was much better. After two days the Scottish army won the battle and the English army left. Robert the Bruce won the Battle of Bannockburn because his army worked together and they believed they could win."

"Thank you for this story, uncle Bruce! Can you tell me something more about Scottish history? It's so interesting!"

"Yes, Rob, I can tell you a lot of stories about Scotland and Scottish history, but not today. It's late already and I'm tired, too. Next time you come and visit me, I'll tell you a story about William Wallace, another brave Scottish man."

[1]brave – *tapfer, mutig*; [2]commander – *Befehlshaber, Kommandeur*; [3]earl – *Graf*; [4]to lead – *anführen*; [5]sword – Schwert; [6]axe – *Axt*

Read the text carefully and complete these sentences.

1. Rob likes to listen to uncle Bruce's stories because ______________________________

   ____

2. The English King doesn't want to talk to Robert the Bruce because ____________________

   ____

   ____

3. Before the battle ______________________________________ Robert the Bruce.

4. The English army lost against the Scots because ______________________________

   ____

   ____

Green Line 2
Vorschläge zur Leistungsmessung
ISBN: 978-3-12-560016-4

4 Writing: An exchange

Next month you're going to visit your partner school in Scotland. The pupils there want to know what you want to see and do while you're in Scotland.
Write an e-mail and say what you'd like to do and why. Here are some ideas:

visit Edinburgh • visit Glasgow • climb Ben Nevis • see Loch Ness • try to play bagpipes • ...

From:	me@funmail.com	Address book
To:	partnerschool@funmail.com	
Subject:	Trip to Scotland	

5 Writing: A story

This is the beginning of a story about a scary castle in Scotland. *Read the text.*

In their summer holiday the three friends Johnny, Charlie and Laura meet in the park, play football or ride their bikes to town. But they want to do something more interesting – a real adventure would be great!
"I don't like this holiday. It's so boring! Everybody has gone away on holiday and there is nothing interesting to do," Johnny said to Charlie and Laura.
"You're right! What do you think about going to the swimming pool? We haven't been there for a long time," Laura answered.
Charlie laughed. "Laura, we went to the swimming pool on Monday. That's two days ago."
"Have you got a better idea?" Laura asked.
"No, I don't know what else we can do. It should be something exciting. We need to tell the others a good story when we go back to school next week. There must be something scary, " Charlie said.
Suddenly Johnny had an idea. "Listen! My brother told me about the ghosts in Stirling Castle. You can hear them at night. Ghosts are scary, aren't they? He told me that people tried to find them, but they've never been seen again. Let's go there at night!"
Charlie was happy. "That's a great idea! I'd love to see everybody's faces when we tell them what we've been doing!"
Laura was very quiet. Then she said, "We'll get into trouble if our parents find out. They'll be very angry!"
"Well, we could say we're going to sleep outside in the tent[1] and then we can go to the castle and find the ghosts," Johnny answered.
Charlie smiled. "That's a good plan! Laura, are you going to come with us or are you being a girl and too scared to go on an adventure?"

[1] tent – *Zelt*

Write an ending for the story. These questions will help you with your text.

- Will Laura go with the boys?
- Will they find the ghosts?
- Will anything happen to the friends? If so, who will come and help them?

Green Line 2
Vorschläge zur Leistungsmessung
ISBN: 978-3-12-560016-4

6 Speaking: Plans

You're in Edinburgh for a long weekend.
Read the information. Work in pairs and discuss what you want to do and when.

Weather report for Scotland

Friday:
12°C

Saturday:
15°C

Sunday:
15°C

Monday:
13°C

What's on?

Ben Nevis Walking Tour: every Friday and Monday, meet in front of the Balmoral Hotel, Princess Street, at 7 am; we expect to be back at 8 pm

Bagpipes concert[1]: Music Hall, Edinburgh, every Friday and Sunday at 7 pm

Guided tour of Edinburgh: daily at 11 am, 1 pm and 3 pm, lasts 2 hours, meet in front of Scott Monument

Loch Ness: visit Loch Ness and find Nessie, every Friday and Sunday, meet in front of the Balmoral Hotel, Princess Street, at 9 am; we expect to be back at 8 pm

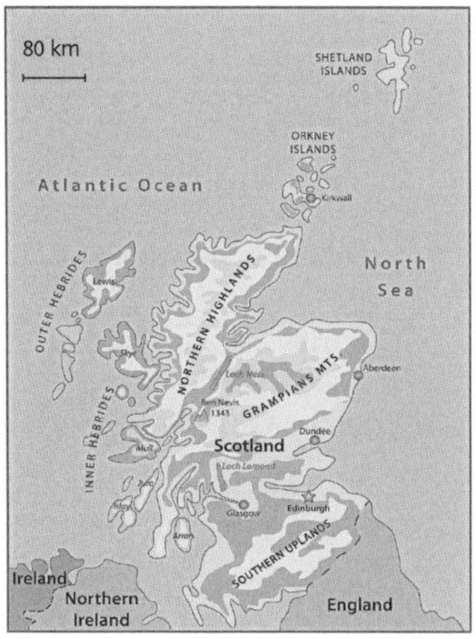

[1]concert ['kɒnsət] – *Konzert*

7 Speaking: A tourist guide

You are a tourist guide and want to show tourists around Edinburgh Castle.
Use the notes and tell them about the castle.

- most famous place
- on Castle Rock, a hill
- over 1,000 years old
- Military Tattoo: every year, August, in front of castle, bagpipes bands, dancing, about 200,000 visitors
- One o'clock gun[1]: every day, 1 pm, people check watch; at first for ships, can be heard from over 3km

[1]gun [gʌn] – *Kanone*

8 Speaking: A holiday picture

You've been to Edinburgh. Now that you are back you want to show some of your holiday pictures to a friend.
Describe the picture. Say where you took it, which event you can see, what the people are wearing and what they are doing.

Green Line 2
Vorschläge zur Leistungsmessung
ISBN: 978-3-12-560016-4

9 Mediation: At the post office

Your whole family is in Scotland on holiday. Your grandma wants to write some postcards to her friends in Germany and needs stamps.
Help her to buy them.

Oma: Ich möchte ein paar Postkarten an Freunde schreiben und brauche noch Briefmarken.

Du: Excuse me, my grandma ______________________________

____

Angestellte: Sure. Where do your friends live? Do you already have the postcards? We've got some over there.

Du: Sie fragt, ______________________________

____

Oma: In Deutschland. Die vier Karten hab ich schon.

Du: ______________________________

Angestellte: OK. Would you like normal stamps or special ones?

Du: ______________________________

Oma: Frage sie bitte, was besondere Briefmarken sind.

Du: ______________________________

Angestellte: Special stamps are more beautiful and a bit more expensive. Some people collect them.

Du: ______________________________

Oma: Die normalen reichen. Wieviel kostet das? Wo werfen wir die Karte ein?

Du: ______________________________

Angestellte: It's 60 pence per stamp. So that's £2.40. The letter box is just outside the building on the right.

Du: ______________________________

Oma: Kannst du sie fragen, wie lange es dauert bis die Karten in Deutschland sind?

Du: ______________________________

Angestellte: They'll take about a week.

Du: ______________________________

Oma: Kannst du dich bitte noch bei der Dame für die Hilfe bedanken?

Du: ______________________________

Green Line 2
Vorschläge zur Leistungsmessung
ISBN: 978-3-12-560016-4

Unit 7 English everywhere

1 Listening: Going abroad

The Cole family wants to go away for a long weekend. They are in the airport.
Listen and tick (✔) the right answer.

1. Tina and her parents want to go to …
   - ☐ Barcelona.
   - ☐ Rome.
   - ☐ Paris.

2. Their flight leaves at …
   - ☐ 10.40.
   - ☐ 2 o'clock.
   - ☐ 8.25.

3. The number of their flight is …
   - ☐ AF 8956.
   - ☐ BA 4711.
   - ☐ FA 8965.

4. They are landing at …
   - ☐ Luis XVI Airport.
   - ☐ Charles de Gaulle Airport.
   - ☐ Nicolas Sarkozy Airport.

5. The first airport announcement says that …
   - ☐ you needn't look after your bags.
   - ☐ you should always keep your bags with you and tell someone if you see a bag without its owner.
   - ☐ you should open other people's bags to find out what is inside.

6. The second announcement says that …
   - ☐ Mr Allister is late for his flight.
   - ☐ Mr Allister has already missed his flight.
   - ☐ Mr Allister is standing at the wrong gate[1].

7. The Cole family must go to gate …
   - ☐ H 78.
   - ☐ L 89.
   - ☐ C 89.

8. Their seats[2] are …
   - ☐ B 27, 28 and 29.
   - ☐ H 8, 9 and 10.
   - ☐ A 15, 16 and 17.

[1]gate – *Flugsteig;* [2]seat – *Platz*

2 Listening: At the travel agent's

Mrs Green needs a holiday. She's at a travel agent's. *Listen and complete the sentences.*
What does she tell her husband (Ehemann) when she comes home?

"I've been to a travel agent's today. I asked for tours around ____________. They had two different ____________: one was ____________ days, and the other one ____________ days. I took the ____________ tour. It starts in ____________ where we have a ____________. It then goes on to ____________, ____________ and Munich. As Munich is near the ____________ we'll go on a hike. I have a ____________ for you, too, but I won't tell you what it is now. The tour ____________ in Cologne. There we'll have time to visit the ____________, the church or go shopping and buy ____________. We'll fly from London on ____________ and come back on ____________. We'll stay in nice ____________ and have ____________ there."

Green Line 2
Vorschläge zur Leistungsmessung
ISBN: 978-3-12-560016-4

3 Reading: Heathrow Airport and the Channel Tunnel

It's Sunday and Emma has just finished her project about London transport – Heathrow Airport and the Channel Tunnel. Here is what she wants to say when she presents it:

My project is about Heathrow and the Channel Tunnel. I got my information from books and the Internet. I chose this project because the holidays are near and a lot of us are going to travel to different countries to enjoy the sun or to visit their friends and family. When we Londoners go away, we can often choose if we want go by plane or take the train through the Channel Tunnel. Most of us have already been to Heathrow Airport and St Pancras Station. But what do we really know about Heathrow and the Channel Tunnel?

Heathrow Airport is one of the biggest airports in the world. You can travel to places all over the world from there and you can meet people from different countries there. Every day about 180,600 passengers use the airport. That is 65.9 million per year. This makes it the second busiest airport in the world after Hartsfield-Jackson Atlanta Airport in the US. Heathrow Airport is in Hillingdon, just outside London. People can easily get there by bike, bus, car, taxi, train or Underground. Did you know that Heathrow has got two runways[1] that are almost 4 km long? There are five terminals where people can catch their flight from. The Queen opened Terminal 5 in 2008. So Heathrow gets bigger and bigger. Every year about half a million planes take off and land. And to make the airport work, about 77,000 people work there. They look after the buildings, work in shops and restaurants, or help when there is a fire.

If you don't want to travel by plane you can go by train through the famous Channel Tunnel – the second longest and deepest[2] underwater tunnel after the Seikan Tunnel in Japan. People built it in the years between 1988 and 1994, but the plans for the tunnel are much older. The idea of an underwater tunnel is over two hundred years old. But in 1802 nobody knew how to build it. Finally a group of people made plans – this took a long time. They needed many different things to make it safe because the water outside pushes against it. After the group had found[3] an answer to all the problems, workers needed six years to build the tunnel and link Great Britain and France. Queen Elizabeth II and the French president[4] François Mitterand opened the tunnel that is 37.9 km long and up to[5] 100 m under water. The Queen travelled on a train called Eurostar and the French president on a French train, called Le Shuttle. Their trains met in the tunnel.
Today the Channel Tunnel is very popular with people – about 16 million passengers use it every year – because it is a fast way of travelling: the new High Speed train can go 300 km / h. That means you can get from London St Pancras to Paris in 2 hours and 20 minutes.

[1]runway – *Landebahn;* [2]deep – *tief;* [3]had found – *gefunden hatte;* [4]president – *Präsident;* [5]up to – *bis zu*

✎ To check whether her classmates have fully understood the text, Emma has prepared a quiz.
Do the quiz:

1. Why did I choose Heathrow Airport and the Channel Tunnel?
2. Where did I get all the information from?
3. Where is Heathrow Airport?
4. How can people get to the airport?
5. Is Heathrow Airport the busiest airport in the world?
6. How many terminals and how many runways does the airport have?
7. What sort of jobs do people do at the airport?
8. Which one has more passengers – Heathrow Airport or the Channel Tunnel?
9. How many years did it take to build the Channel Tunnel?
10. When did people first talk about an underwater tunnel and why did they not try to build it?
11. Did the same English person open Terminal 5 and the Channel Tunnel?
12. How long is the tunnel and how deep is it?
13. Is it the longest and largest tunnel in the world?
14. How fast can the High Speed train travel?
15. How long does it take to travel from London to Paris?

Green Line 2
Vorschläge zur Leistungsmessung
ISBN: 978-3-12-560016-4

4 Writing: Visit Britain

You are working on the project "Visit Britain" in your English class. You have already found some information about the Channel Tunnel and Heathrow Airport. Now you want to write the texts for your poster.

Write a short text about Heathrow Airport and the Channel Tunnel. The pictures and facts will help you.

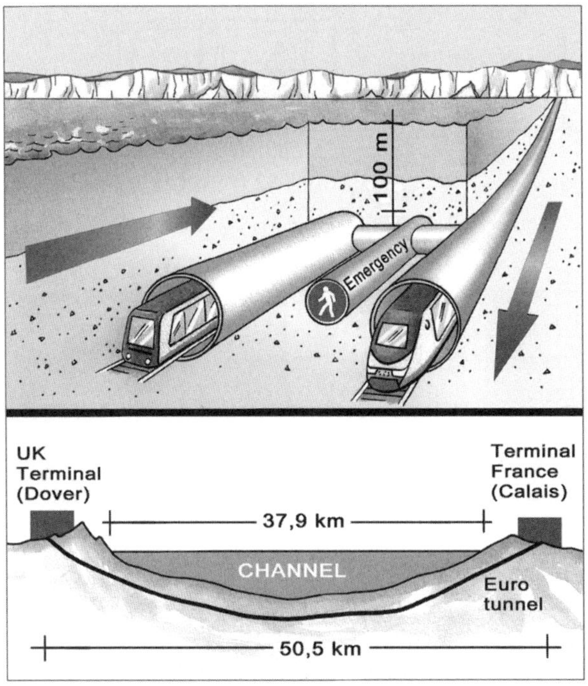

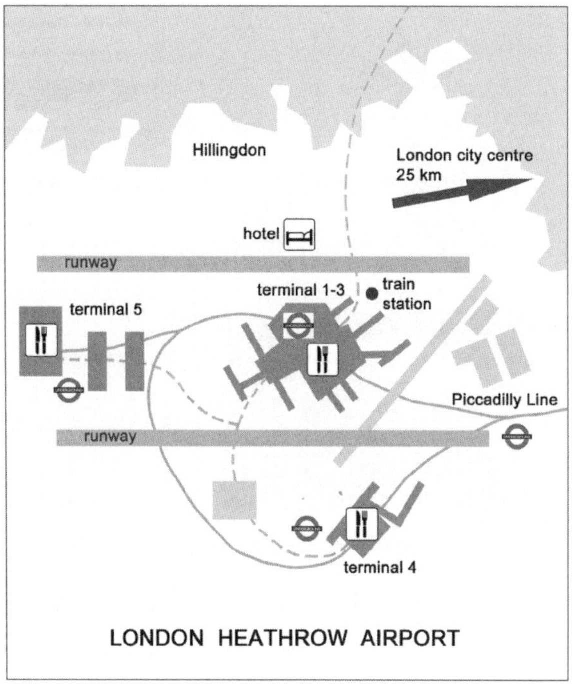

5 Writing: Holidays

Write a letter / e-mail to your friend in England about your last holiday, class trip or weekend trip. Say …

- where you travelled to.
- who you went with.
- which form of transport you used to get there.
- how long it took to get there.
- how long you stayed there.
- where you slept.
- what you saw and did there.
- what you liked the most and what you didn't like.
- whether[1] you'd like to go there again

[1]whether – *ob*

6 Writing: My tips

Your friend from England wants to visit Germany. He / She has asked you for some tips.
Write an e-mail and tell your friend which five places he / she should visit and why.
Write 120 to 150 words.

ISBN: 978-3-12-560016-4

7 Speaking: A visit to the UK

The summer holidays are about to start. Together with your best friend you want to travel to the UK. Each (Jeder) of you can spend £600. You want to see as much as you can, but enjoy the sun, too.
Work in pairs. Discuss your travel plans and come to an agreement.

a) *How do you want to get to the UK? What are the pros and cons?*

£39.98
1 hour 30 minutes

£65
8 hours 30 minutes

£89.50
13 hours 12 minutes

b) *Which part of Britain do you want to go to?*

Cornwall

London

Scotland

Wales

c) *What do you want to see and do there? Here are some ideas:*

English course

surf

castle

hike

abseil

d) *Where do you want to sleep? Why?*

hotel	youth hostel[1]	host family	Bed & Breakfast	tent[2]
£34.50 per person	£15.00 per person	£15.00 per person	£32.00 per person	£5.00

[1]youth hostel – *Jugendherberge;* [2]tent – *Zelt*

e) *What do you want to take to Britain? Here are some ideas:*

wellies

travel guide

dictionary

sunglasses

?

f) *Where do you want to eat? Here are some ideas:*

restaurant

snack bar

own food

Green Line 2
Vorschläge zur Leistungsmessung
ISBN: 978-3-12-560016-4

8 Mediation: On the plane

You are on a plane. An old lady who doesn't understand very much English is sitting next to you.
Tell her what the stewardess is saying in German.

Stewardess: Welcome on board our airplane. Please stay in your seats[1] during the flight and have your seatbelt fastened. Your life-jacket is under your seat and if you have any questions, please ask us.

Ältere Dame: Hast du verstanden, was die Stewardess gesagt hat?

Du: Ja, klar. Sie hat gesagt, dass ______________________

____

____

Ältere Dame: Da vorne kommt die Stewardess. Kannst du Sie bitte nach einem Glas Wasser fragen? Ich habe ziemlichen Durst.

Du: Excuse me! This lady doesn't speak English. ______________________

____

Stewardess: Of course. We'll bring water, tea and coffee for all passengers in a minute.

Ältere Dame: Was hat sie gesagt?

Du: ______________________

Ältere Dame: Wenn Sie zurückkommt, kannst du sie dann bitte auch nach einer deutschen Zeitschrift fragen?

Du: Natürlich mach ich das!

Stewardess: Does she want coffee, tea or water?

Du: ______________________

Ältere Dame: Ich nehme einen Tee und ein Wasser, wenn das geht. Und fragst du sie bitte nach der Zeitschrift?

Du: ______________________

Stewardess: Here is the water, a cup of tea and a magazine. Is there anything else I can do for the lady?

Du: ______________________

Ältere Dame: Nein danke. Vielleicht später.

Du: ______________________

[1]seat – *Platz, Sitz*

Green Line 2
Vorschläge zur Leistungsmessung
ISBN: 978-3-12-560016-4

Unit 1 Back to school

1 Wordwise: School words

Find the words and write them down.

1. The tutor groups in Year 8 meet for this on Monday mornings. ______________________
2. This plan shows pupils which lessons they have and when. ______________________
3. The German word for this is “Schulfach”. ______________________
4. Pupils at Thomas Tallis have five of these every day – four in the morning and one after lunch. ______________________
5. The time when lessons stop and pupils can play in the playground. ______________________
6. Pupils at most British schools wear this. At TTS it’s black and blue. ______________________

2 Wordwise: Mixed bag

At morning tutorial, Mrs Carter asks the children about their summer holidays.
Complete the missing words.

Mrs Carter: It’s nice to see you back at sch_____, girls and boys. Did you all enj_____ your holidays? Emma, I know that you we_____ in Cornwall. Did you have a good time?

Emma: Yes, we did. The first week wasn’t very good because it rained alm_____ every day. But in the second week the rain st_____ and the sun came out again. Th_____ we sat on the beach and a_____ ice-cream every day!

Mrs Carter: Sounds great. Now, Terry, ple_____ tell us what you did in the holidays.

Terry: Well, we di_____ go on holiday this year, Mrs Carter. My par_____ wanted to do some things in the house. So we st_____ at home and I helped them. My dad and I bui_____ a table for my shed. But we didn’t stay at home every day. One after_____ we visited the zoo and I r_____ on an elephant. And another day we w_____ to the London Aquarium. We s_____ some beautiful fish there. But some of them were very sc_____.

Mrs Carter: Well, so you had a good time at home, too, Terry. Now, Lisa, tell us about your holidays. Wh_____ did you do?

Lisa: We took our dog to a holiday park in Wales. Barker loved it. Every day he found some new doggy friends on the beach and he pl_____ with them. And I met some great new friends, t_____.

Green Line 2
Vorschläge zur Leistungsmessung
ISBN: 978-3-12-560016-4

3 Language: Rob's first day at TTS

Fill in the simple past form of the verb in brackets (…).

On Monday morning Rob got up (get up) early. It __________ (be) his first day at his new school. He __________ (wear) his new uniform and his new shoes. When he __________ (arrive) at TTS, Mrs Carter and Lisa __________ (meet) him at the entrance. "Welcome[1] to Thomas Tallis," they __________ (say) and __________ (smile).

At 8.40 morning tutorial __________ (start). First Mrs Carter __________ (take) the register. Then she __________ (ask) the children about their holidays. Rob__________ (tell) the class a funny story, and all the children __________ (laugh).

After morning tutorial there __________ (be) two lessons before break, then another two before lunch at ten past one. At lunchtime Rob __________ (go) to the cafeteria. He __________ (buy) spaghetti and he __________ (sit) next to his new friend, Lisa. When his mother __________ (collect) him in the car at 3.20, Rob __________ (look) very happy.

[1]welcome – *Willkommen*

4 Language: Lots of questions

Fill in did, was *or* were *and give the right short answer.*

1. ________ Rob enjoy his first day at TTS? – (+) Yes, ____________________
2. ________ the first lesson after break Technology? – (-) No, ____________________
3. ________ there two breaks in the morning? – (-) ____________________
4. ________ Lisa have lunch in the cafeteria? – (+) ____________________
5. ________ the pupils get a lot of homework? – (-) ____________________
6. ________ you late for school this morning? – ____________________

5 Language: The first day

Make questions. Use when, what time, where, what, who, how many *or* why.

Here is one example: Mrs Carter gave her tutor group <u>their new timetable</u>. –
What did Mrs Carter give her tutor group?

1. Morning tutorial started <u>at 8.40</u>.
2. Lisa and Rob played football <u>in the playground</u> at break.
3. Rob ate <u>spaghetti</u> for lunch.
4. There were <u>two</u> lessons before morning break.
5. Rob did his homework <u>before he watched TV</u>.
6. He went to bed early <u>because he was tired</u>.
7. <u>Rob</u> was very happy.

Green Line 2
Vorschläge zur Leistungsmessung
ISBN: 978-3-12-560016-4

6 Language: But ...

Look at the example. Make sentences. Use the simple past form of the verb.

1. Rob – (not / wear) – his jeans – to school. He – (wear) – his new school uniform.

   Rob didn't wear his jeans to school. He wore his new school uniform.

2. He – (not / go) – to school – by bike. He – (go) – to school – by car.
3. The first lesson – (not / be) – German. It – (be) – Technology.
4. Rob – (not / have) – lunch – in the classroom. He – (have) – lunch – in the cafeteria.
5. School – (not / finish) – after the last lesson. It – (finish) – after afternoon tutorial.

7 Language: The weekend

On Monday morning, Lisa meets Mrs Carter in the school playground. She asks Lisa about her weekend. *Fill in the simple past form of the verb in brackets (...).*

Mrs Carter: Hello, Lisa. ____________ (you / have) a nice weekend?

Lisa: Yes, thank you, Mrs Carter. I ________ (have) a great weekend. On Saturday Terry, Sam, Emma and I ________ (play) football together in the park, and on Sunday we all ________ (go) to the zoo. Terry's dad ________ (take) us there in his taxi.

Mrs Carter: Oh, that ________ (be) very nice of Mr Jackson. They've got a new baby gorilla at London Zoo. ________ (you / see) it?

Lisa: No, we ________ (not see) the baby gorilla because there ________ (be) too many people there and we ________ (not want) to wait. But we ________ (see) the new panda bears[1]. They ________ (be) very sweet. And we ________ (ride) on an elephant, too, but that ________ (be) scary because the elephant ________ (stop) suddenly and we almost fell off[2]!

Mrs Carter: Oh dear! But you ________ (survive) your trip to the zoo and you ________ (enjoy) your weekend. ____________ (you / find) time to do your German homework, too?

Lisa: German homework? ____________ (it / be) for today, Mrs Carter?

Mrs Carter: Yes, Lisa. I ________ (tell) you on Friday that you must write down the new words on page 164 in your vocabulary books and learn them for today.

Lisa: Oh, that's OK, Mrs Carter. I ________ (do) that last week.

[1]panda bear – *Panda*; [2]fell off – *sind herunter gefallen*

Green Line 2
Vorschläge zur Leistungsmessung
ISBN: 978-3-12-560016-4

Unit 2 Welcome to London

1 Wordwise: Words

Look at the pictures and find the words.

1. A guidebook

4. ______

2. ______

5. ______

3. ______

6. six

2 Wordwise: Opposites

Look at the example. Write down the opposite.

1. to start ______
2. to arrive ______
3. to get off ______
4. to laugh ______
5. better than ______
6. the longest ______
7. colder than ______
8. the cheapest ______

3 Language: one and ones

Complete the sentences. Use one *or* ones.

1. There are two pens on the table – (ein schwarzer und ein blauer).

______

2. The house has got three bathrooms – (zwei große und ein kleines).

______

3. Jenny has got two schoolbags – (eine alte und eine neue).

______

4. Which of those girls over there is your sister? – (Die mit den roten Haaren).

______

Green Line 2
Vorschläge zur Leistungsmessung
ISBN: 978-3-12-560016-4

4 Language: have got and have

a) *Underline the verb forms. Write down the negative form.*

1. The Taylors <u>have got</u> two cars. haven't got ______
2. The Taylors <u>have</u> two cars. ______
3. Lisa has a travelcard. ______
4. The girls had lunch in the cafeteria. ______
5. They are having a good time. ______
6. Grandma has got a dog. ______

b) *Make questions. Use* what, when, where *or* how many.
Here is one example: Where have the Brooks got a flat? or: Where do the Brooks have a flat?
– The Brooks have got a flat over a computer shop.

1. ______
– They have a small flat <u>in Holburne Road</u>.

2. ______
– It has got <u>two</u> bedrooms.

3. ______
– Emma's dad has <u>a computer shop</u>.

4. ______
– <u>Two years ago</u> they had a house in Bristol.

5 Language: An unlucky day for some

Yesterday was Friday, the thirteenth. Read what happened to these people.
Fill in the correct form of the verbs in brackets (…). Use the simple past or the past progressive.

1. Katie and Jenny ______ (sit) on a bus when the driver ______ (stop) suddenly and two passengers ______ (fall) on top of them.
2. David ______ (hurt) his hand while he ______ (get off) the Tube. He ______ (catch) it in the door of the train.
3. James ______ (lose) his mobile phone while he ______ (run) to the bus stop.
4. While Harry ______ (wait) for a train, he ______ (see) his girlfriend with another boy. They ______ (hold) hands and they ______ (kiss).
5. While Mrs Simpson ______ (cross) the road, a car ______ (come) around the corner and almost ______ (run) into her.

Green Line 2
Vorschläge zur Leistungsmessung
ISBN: 978-3-12-560016-4

Klett

6 Language: Can we go to Hamleys?

Hanna, a German girl from Frankfurt, is visiting the Taylors. They are talking about their plans for the day. *Fill in the missing words.*

Jade: Can we go to Hamleys today, Mum?

Mrs Taylor: Um. Yes. That's a ________________ (gute) idea, Jade.

Hanna: What's Hamleys?

Mrs Taylor: It's a ________________ (großes) toy shop in London. It's ________________ (der berühmteste) toy shop in Britain and ________________ (der älteste) one in the world.

Mr Taylor: That's right. But don't forget, Hamleys is one of ________________ (der beliebtesten) shops in London, too. And you know what that means, don't you? – The queues are ________________ (schrecklich) there! Listen! I've got a ________________ (bessere) idea. Let's go to the toy shop in Greenwich. They have ________________ (schöne) things, too, and they are ________________ (nicht so teuer wie) the toys at Hamleys.

Jade: Oh, Dad! The toy shop in Greenwich is ________________ (langweilig). The toys at Hamleys are much ________________ (aufregender). Some of the monsters there are ________________ (unheimlicher als) the dinosaurs at the Natural History Museum!

Mrs Taylor: Well, of course Hamleys is much ________________ (größer als) the shop in Greenwich. But Dad's right, Jade. Saturday really is a ________________ (schlecht) day for shopping there. Let's go there on Monday afternoon when it isn't so ________________ (voll).

Green Line 2
Vorschläge zur Leistungsmessung
ISBN: 978-3-12-560016-4

Unit 3 Pocket money

1 Wordwise: A menu

What can you eat in the snack bar? *Look at the pictures and write down the menu.*

1 
2 
3 
4 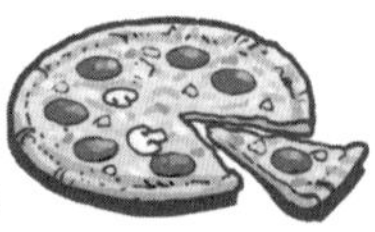
5 
6 

Menu

1 ______________________________ £6.60

2 ______________________________ £3.90

3 ______________________________ £4.20

4 ______________________________ £5.60

5 ______________________________ £3.40

6 ______________________________ £2.30

2 Wordwise: Shopping

Lisa explains where she usually goes shopping. *Find the missing words and put them in.*

I like going … (1) because I don't want to save my pocket … (2). The shop … (3) at 'Street Style' are very nice. I like all the … (4) there. They look great and they aren't too expensive. The shop has nice … (5) rooms where I spend a lot of time.

3 Language: Question tags

a) Tina and Jody are looking at things on the Internet. *Fill in the correct question tags.*

Tina: Well, this green skirt looks nice, ___________? Oh, you don't like green, ___________?

Jody: No, I don't. What trainers do they have?

Tina: Hm, let's see. Look. But I think the trainers we saw in the shop yesterday were nicer, ___________?

Jody: Yes, you're right.

Green Line 2
Vorschläge zur Leistungsmessung
ISBN: 978-3-12-560016-4

b) Sam and Terry are in a shop that sells mobiles, games and CDs.
Fill in the correct question tags.

Sam: Wow! Look at this mobile phone! It's expensive, ____________?

Terry: Yes, the things they sell in this shop are very expensive. The CDs are expensive, too.

The ones we saw in the shopping centre on Tuesday were much better, ____________?

Sam: You're right. Can we go and have a look at the computer games?

Terry: Sure, but you bought a game on Tuesday, ____________?

Sam: Yes, but look, this one sounds interesting. But I haven't got much money.

You can't lend me £5, ____________?

4 Language: 's or s'

Use the correct genitive form, for example: ***Jenny's*** *new computer has got a lot of games on it. (Jenny)*

1. This is ____________________ new mobile phone. (Lisa)
2. ____________________ house is beautiful. (our friends)
3. ____________________ new CD player doesn't sound very nice. (my friend)
4. ____________________ skirts are beautiful. (the girls)
5. That's ____________________ bag. (Tracy)
6. That pupil over there is in ____________________ class. (Mr Colin)
7. Hey, stop that. Don't take other ____________________ food! (people)
8. Where is the ____________________ changing room? (women)

5 Language: What are they going to do?

Write down what the people are going to do this afternoon.

1. Carol is going to read a book. (read)

2. Lisa and Emma ______________________________. (buy)

3. Karen ______________________________. (answer)

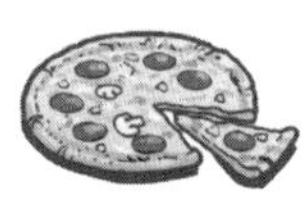

4. The friends ______________________________. (eat)

5. Mrs Taylor ______________________________. (listen)
6. Mr Taylor ______________________________. (wash)

Green Line 2
Vorschläge zur Leistungsmessung
ISBN: 978-3-12-560016-4

6 Language: The weekend

a) Terry asks Sam questions about his weekend plans.
Write down Terry's questions and Sam's answers.

Terry:	Sam:
Are you ______	visit grandma and grandad
______	do homework
______	not go to the cinema
______	play computer games

b) Now Sam asks Terry questions about what he did last weekend.
Write down Sam's questions and Terry's answers.

Sam:	Terry:
Did ______	help mum in the kitchen
______	watch TV
______	write an e-mail
______	not spend money on sweets

7 Language: The shopping list

Mr Jackson and Terry are making a shopping list before they go to the supermarket to buy the things they need for the weekend. *Complete the dialogue.*

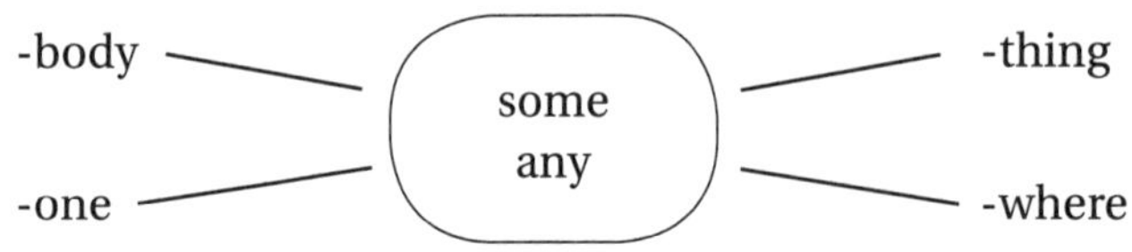

Mr Jackson: We need ______ bacon and eggs for breakfast. Is there ______ else[1] we need for breakfast?

Terry: Hm, we haven't got ______ cornflakes. I think we need ______ milk and bread, too. There wasn't ______ this morning. ______ must have finished it.

Mr Jackson: I don't like cornflakes, but it's OK. And we need ______ for lunch. Have you got an idea?

Terry: Let's get ______ fish and chips for lunch.

Mr Jackson: Yes, but we can't buy them at the supermarket. We need to go ______ else.

[1]else – *sonst, anders*

Green Line 2
Vorschläge zur Leistungsmessung
ISBN: 978-3-12-560016-4

Unit 4 Who wants to be a star?

1 Wordwise: Who wants to be a star?

Lisa talks about stars. *Find the missing words and fill them in.*

Before a band can perform well[1] they must … (1) a lot. When they are happy with their music, they can go to an … (2), and if they are good, they can perform on … (3). Sometimes it is good to have … (4) dancers and … (5) in a band. To become more popular, they can even go on … (6), sing on TV or on the … (7). Then they can make … (8).

[1]well – *gut*

2 Language: Past participles

Fill in the missing past participles.

take – took – ___________	talk – talked – ___________	see – saw – ___________
fall – fell – ___________	leave – left – ___________	check – checked – ___________
have – had – ___________	learn – learnt – ___________	meet – met – ___________
find – found – ___________	win – won – ___________	buy – bought – ___________
say – said – ___________	get – got – ___________	sell – sold – ___________
become – became – ___________	do – did – ___________	write – wrote – ___________
lose – lost – ___________	sing – sang – ___________	wake up – woke up – ___________

Green Line 2
Vorschläge zur Leistungsmessung
ISBN: 978-3-12-560016-4

3 Language: What have they done?

Find the right phrase and write down what they have done.

write invitation cards | jump through window | build sand castle | walk the dog

wake up | do the homework

1. Lisa has just walked the dog.
2. Lisa and Jade ______________________.

3. The children ______________________.
4. Terry ______________________.

5. Tiger ______________________.
6. Tom ______________________.

4 Language: Have you ever …?

Terry prepares questions for his classmate. *Write them down. Start with 'Have you ever…'.*

London?

have a pet?

sing a song in front of lots of people?

play basketball?

help your dad in the garden?

lose your money?

go shopping with your mum?

invite all your friends to your house?

Green Line 2
Vorschläge zur Leistungsmessung
ISBN: 978-3-12-560016-4

5 Language: just or not yet

Write a sentence for each situation. Use just *or* not yet*.*

the bus – leave

the train – go

she – go out

he – open – present

they – finish – their homework

it – stop – raining

6 Language: Simple past or present perfect

Find the right verb forms: simple past or present perfect.

Tina: Do you know James's cousin?

Jody: I saw ________ (see) her three times but I've never spoken ________ (never speak) to her. ________ (you / ever / speak) to her?

Tina: Yes. I ________ (meet) her at a party last week. She's very nice.

Mrs Green: ________ (you / ever / be) to New York?

Mr Barton: Yes, we ________ (go) there on holiday two years ago.

Mrs Green: ________ (you / have) a good time?

Mr Barton: Yes, I really ________ (enjoy) it.

Jade: Where's Lisa? ________ (you / see) her?

Ben: Yes, she ________ (go) to her friend's house a few minutes ago.

Jade: And Mum?

Ben: I don't know. I ________ (not / see) her yet.

Sam: ________ (you / ever / have) anything interesting to eat?

Lisa: Yes, I ________ (have) some dog food. I ________ (think) it ________ (be) for me.

Green Line 2
Vorschläge zur Leistungsmessung
ISBN: 978-3-12-560016-4

Unit 5 Fit for Life

1 Wordwise: Sports

Find ten words about sports and put them under the right title.

X	A	E	G	H	J	K	L	E	I	B	A	M
C	R	O	C	K	C	L	I	M	B	I	N	G
E	X	T	P	S	Y	N	F	I	S	Z	O	D
R	T	R	A	Q	B	R	E	T	W	Y	R	J
T	H	A	E	L	F	E	J	S	I	X	A	G
H	J	I	R	T	W	P	A	P	M	T	K	F
U	U	N	O	G	C	O	C	Z	M	V	Q	J
L	D	E	B	I	A	R	K	E	E	D	H	E
D	O	R	I	E	N	T	E	E	R	I	N	G
F	N	M	C	I	O	E	T	R	L	Y	C	I
Q	R	P	S	U	E	R	F	J	K	W	Q	N

Sports	Equipment	People

2 Wordwise: Body parts

Write down the body parts.

Green Line 2
Vorschläge zur Leistungsmessung
ISBN: 978-3-12-560016-4

3 Wordwise: Adjectives

Complete the sentences with the right adjective.

dhar • wegoveriht • hvyea • recaulf • singbeamrras • endyfril • grany • thehyal

When I was a child, I was ______________. I ate too much and didn't do much sport. It was ______________. The doctor was ______________ with my parents. Later he was always nice and ______________, but on that day he wasn't happy at all. The doctor said I should try swimming. I went swimming the next day and loved it right away. After that I ate more ______________ food, too, and I got fit very quickly. It wasn't ______________ for me because I loved swimming so much. Now I'm an Olympic swimmer, but I must still be ______________ with what I eat because I can get too ______________ very quickly.

4 Language: An interview

a) *Read the interview and complete the questions.*

Interviewer: Where ____

Alice: I come from Scotland, but I've lived here for ten years.

Interviewer: Who ____

Alice: A judo teacher taught me to do judo.

Interviewer: Who ____

Alice: I train with my friends. They love judo, too.

Interviewer: What ______________________ when you're fighting in a judo competition?

Alice: I don't think about anything – my head is empty.

Interviewer: What ____

Alice: Oh, my friends make me feel happier, but judo is very important for me, too.

b) *What other three questions would you like to ask Alice? You can use these notes for help.*

____

____

____

____

help – keep fit • more important – school / go swimming • make angry – make happy • favourite food • …

Green Line 2
Vorschläge zur Leistungsmessung
ISBN: 978-3-12-560016-4

5 Language: School reports

Read the school reports (Zeugnisse) and complete the sentences with the right adverbs.

hard • well • in a friendly way • beautiful • nervously • carefully • quietly

Pupil: Ellis Thompson Class: 8B

Overall:
Ellis is a very popular pupil in class 8B and is always friendly to the other pupils. He is a hard worker but he must be more careful when he writes.

Pupil: Zoe Franck Class: 8B

Overall:
Zoe is a quiet girl and she is a good worker. She is often nervous when she answers questions.

Pupil: Luke Miller Class: 8B

Overall:
Luke is very good at music and has got a beautiful voice. He shows that he is a very fast learner in his guitar lessons at school.

1. Ellis talks to other pupils _______________.
   He works _______________.
   He must write more _______________.
2. Zoe sits _______________ in class. She answers questions _______________, but works _______________.
3. Luke sings _______________. He's learning to play the guitar very _______________.

6 Language: My family

For her homework Emily wrote about her family. *Complete the sentences about her family.*

1. My brother, Ben, is younger than me, but he can run faster. But our dog can run even faster than Ben.

   Emily's dog runs ____.

2. I must work hard for school, but my brother doesn't need to work much – that's unfair. My parents work hard, of course, but my poor Aunt Audrey works day and night.

   Emily works _______________ than her brother, but her Aunt Audrey works _______________.

3. Nobody can sing well in my family. Our dog is a terrible singer, of course, but my brother is worse. And my mum? Everybody leaves the house when she starts to sing.

   Emily's brother sings _______________ than the dog but her mum sings _______________.

4. In our house my mum usually does the cooking. My dad can't cook at all. But we always want to eat at my aunt's house because she is a very good cook.

   Emily's mum cooks _______________ than her dad, but her aunt cooks _______________.

5. And what can I do? I can paint beautiful pictures. I don't know how I learnt to do it because my parents can't paint at all. The bad thing is that my brother can paint even better than me.

   Emily can paint _______________ than her parents but her brother paints _______________.

Green Line 2
Vorschläge zur Leistungsmessung
ISBN: 978-3-12-560016-4

Unit 6 In Scotland

1 Wordwise: The bag

Complete Rob's e-mail to his uncle in Scotland. Use the words from the box.

so • as soon as • because • but • although • after • when • and

Dear Uncle Bruce,

____________ we arrived back from Scotland, I went back to school the next day. On the first day ____________ I walked home from school, I found a bag on the street corner. I didn't know whose[1] bag it was ____________ I didn't want to leave it there. I looked around ____________ there was nobody in the street that I could ask. ____________ I took the bag home with me. I wasn't sure if I could open it ____________ it was somebody else's[2]. ____________ I really wanted to know what was in the bag, I didn't open it. ____________ Mum came home in the evening, I told her about the bag. She said that we could open the bag ____________ we needed to find out whose bag it was ____________ take it to the person. ____________ we opened the bag. It was a sports bag. There were trainers, trousers, a T-shirt ____________ a bottle of water in it. ____________ we didn't find the name in the trainers, we found a name inside the T-shirt. It was our neighbour's boy's bag. Mum told me to call the boy ____________ tell him that we've got his bag. He was happy ____________ said, 'Thank you, I'll come and pick it up'.

[1]whose – *wessen;* [2]else – *sonst, irgend*

2 Wordwise: if or when

Mr Travelot has to (muss) go to Berlin and work there. He has never been there and so he starts to make plans for his trip. *Complete the sentences. Use* if *or* when.

______ I arrive at the airport[1], I must find a train into the city. But what ______ I don't find a train station at the airport? Then I can take a taxi. ______ I find a train that takes me to the city I can use my map to find the hotel[2]. I can ask the people on the street ______ I have any problems. I'll stay in Berlin for three weeks and work there. At the weekends, ______ I have some free time, I want to see all the sights in Berlin. I'd like to climb to the top of the "Reichstag" ______ the weather is good. But ______ the "Reichstag" is too full and I can't go upstairs, I'll try to find the "Fernsehturm". After that I'd like to visit one of the museums and see some old pictures ______ I'm not too tired. ______ they have a shop there I can buy a nice souvenir for my son.

[1]airport – *Flughafen;* [2]hotel – *Hotel*

Green Line 2
Vorschläge zur Leistungsmessung
ISBN: 978-3-12-560016-4

3 Language: Weather report

Have a look at the weather chart (Karte) for Great Britain.
Write the weather report for Tuesday. Use the correct tense.

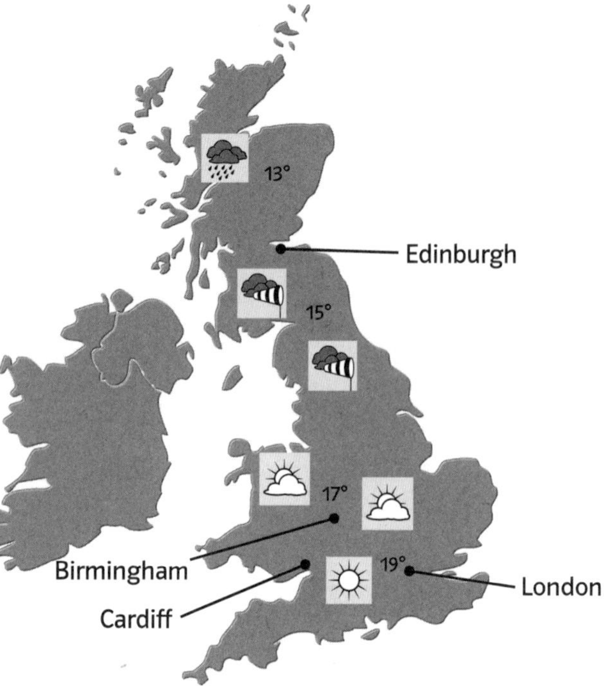

4 Language: Where is my lunchbox?

Miss Carter's class is on a class trip. They're having a lunch break, but some pupils can't find their lunchbox (Brotbüchse). *Complete the sentences with the right possessive pronoun.*

Lisa: Emma can't find her lunchbox. She knows that she has an orange, so the lunchbox she has now can't be ___________ because there's an apple in it.

Rob: Maybe she's got ___________. I love apples and my mum always gives me one in the morning. Look at Terry, I think he has ___________!

Emma: Hm, yes. Terry is lucky. He's got ___________. But where is my lunchbox? Maybe it's the one Sam has got.

Rob: Hey, Sam, I think you've got Emma's lunchbox! She's still looking for ___________.

Sam: Maybe. There's an orange, a cheese sandwich and a pack of sweets in it.

Emma: Oh, it's ___________ then. Mum gave me some sweets for all of us. But Lisa and James are still looking for ___________. Let's help them. What colour are ___________?

Lisa & Rob: ___________ are the blue and the green boxes in the back of the bus. Thanks, we've just found them.

Green Line 2
Vorschläge zur Leistungsmessung
ISBN: 978-3-12-560016-4

5 Language: The purse

Sam and Terry are in the park. They find a purse (Geldbörse) with lots of money and credit cards in it under a tree. They don't know what to do with it. *Complete the dialogue with the ideas from the box.*

police know what to do • keep all the money • owner very unhappy • leave purse under the tree • happy owner gives them something as a 'thank you' • owner come back

Terry: What do you think we should do with the purse?

Sam: Hm, I'm not sure. If we take it with us, ______________________________

Terry: Yes, but we can buy a new football and new trainers, ______________________________

Sam: That would be great. But maybe we should just leave the purse under the tree. ____________

______________________________, he'll be very happy to find his money and the credit cards.

Terry: But ______________________________, somebody else may steal it.

Sam: You're right. I've got an idea. If we take it to the police station, ______________________________

____

Terry: Yes, let's do that. And if we're very lucky, ______________________________

____

6 Language: A rainy weekend

Complete the sentences with the right future tense.

Boy: Mum, the weather report says that it __________ rain this afternoon. So we can't go on our hike. We wanted to walk to the castle because they __________ show "The Battle of Bannockburn", remember?

Mum: Oh dear! Look at those dark clouds – the rain __________ (not) wait, that's for sure.

Boy: So what can we do? Do you think there __________ be lots of people at the swimming pool?

Mum: I'm sure there __________ be. I know: a friend at work __________ be at the museum with her son this afternoon. We could go with her.

Boy: A museum? No way! How about shopping? I need new shoes next winter because my old ones __________ be too small then. And we __________ (not) get wet in the shops.

Mum: Let's talk about this later. It's ten to ten. We __________ be late for your riding lesson.

Green Line 2
Vorschläge zur Leistungsmessung
ISBN: 978-3-12-560016-4

Unit 7 English everywhere

1 Wordwise: Travel words

Look at the words in the box and sort them. You'll need some words more than once (einmal).

ferry • baggage • flight • plane • to take off • passport • customs • shuttle • terminal • train
announcement • ship • map • platform • bus • helicopter • coast • sea • ocean • to land

airport	harbour	station	what people take on trips

2 Wordwise: Verbs

a) *Find the infinitive form of 12 verbs. Then write down their past forms.*

S	E	N	D	J	C	H	G
P	T	W	S	H	A	K	E
E	A	T	Q	I	L	D	A
A	B	S	X	D	L	T	E
K	R	B	L	E	E	D	D
N	E	R	I	D	E	F	H
O	A	M	I	S	S	Y	I
P	K	K	F	I	G	H	T

infinitive	simple past	past participle
1.		
2.		
3.		
4.		
5.		
6.		
7.		
8.		
9.		
10.		
11.		
12.		

b) *Choose five verbs and use them in a short dialogue.*

Green Line 2
Vorschläge zur Leistungsmessung
ISBN: 978-3-12-560016-4

3 Language: Be polite!

You are in Great Britain where you are staying with a host family.
What do you say in these situations? Remember to be polite. You needn't use all the words.

shall • may • could • couldn't • can • can't • should • shouldn't

1. Du willst wissen, wo sich ein Briefkasten befindet.	1. I've written a postcard to my parents. ______ you tell me where I can find a letter box to send it?
2. Du hast Hunger, aber es gibt erst in einer Stunde Abendessen.	2. I know it's not time for the evening meal yet, but I'm hungry. ______ I have some bread before we eat together?
3. Die Katze deiner Gastfamilie sitzt vor der Tür und möchte raus.	3. I think your cat wants to go outside. ______ I open the door and let her out?
4. Am Frühstückstisch steht der Käse weit von dir entfernt.	4. ______ I have the cheese, please?
5. Einige Schüler wollen am Dienstag ins Kino gehen. Du möchtest mit und willst wissen, wann du spätestens zurück sein sollst.	5. Some pupils want to go to the cinema on Tuesday. ______ I go with them? – Sure. – What time ______ I be back? – At 9 o'clock at the latest.
6. Du möchtest ein paar Souvenirs kaufen, aber konntest keinen Laden finden. Um zu einem Laden zu kommen, will dir die Gastfamilie das Busticket bezahlen.	6. ______ you tell me where I find a souvenir shop? I ______ find one anywhere near us. – There isn't one near. You need to take the bus, but I'll pay for your ticket. – No, thanks. You really ______ pay for it.

4 Language: A project

Complete the sentences with the simple past or present perfect. (Watch out for the signal word.)

For the last 15 years the teachers at Thomas Tallis School ______ (always / do) a project with the pupils in Year 8 – this year, too. So last week Emma ______ (tell) her tutor that she'd like to do a project about Heathrow Airport because she ______ (pick up) some friends from the airport last month and ______ (think) it was interesting. Emma ______ (not be) on a plane yet, but she would like to fly to another country some day. She needs lots of information for her project, but she ______ (just / start) to look for it. Yesterday she ______ (look) on the Internet where she ______ (find) a lot of information.

Green Line 2
Vorschläge zur Leistungsmessung
ISBN: 978-3-12-560016-4

5 Language: After the first day

Christian is on a language learning holiday in England. He is staying with a host family and goes to summer school. After his first day at school his host family asks him a lot of questions.
Write six questions and what you think his answers are. Are his answers positive or negative?

Did	you your classmates anybody your teacher	show ask give talk take eat meet welcome tell get have	home lunch with you books you for your name nice people where to go where to find homework library fun

6 Language: The fortune-teller

You go to see a fortune-teller (Wahrsager) because you want to know what the future holds for you.
Write six questions and the answers you would hope for or not like to hear. Here are some ideas:

what when where who why will how many	friends / brother / sister children I car / bike cat / dog job / house presents	get do give have be famous drive live

7 Language: An interview

You've just started to work for a popular German youth magazine. You've been asked to do an interview with Robert Pattinson, the famous actor from the vampire (Vampir) films.
To prepare (vorbereiten) for the interview, you write down your questions about Robert's life.

1. Thanks for coming to Berlin for this interview. (ever / be to Germany / to make a film)

   ____

2. You played Edward Cullen in the vampire films. (ever / read / other vampire stories)

   ____

3. There are a lot of stunts in your films. Do you do them yourself or (ever / need / stuntman[1])

   ____

4. As an actor you must learn the lines. (ever / forget text and say something funny)

   ____

5. You play in a lot of films, but (ever / perform / on stage in a theatre)

   ____

[1]stuntman – *Stuntman*

Green Line 2
Vorschläge zur Leistungsmessung
ISBN: 978-3-12-560016-4

Lösungen

Unit 1 Back to school

1 Listening: Back at school

Either:
Italian food, surfing, abseiling, picnic, holidays on a farm, the rain in Cornwall, holidays with grandma and granddad, History

Or:
1. Jody, Tina and Mr Barton are talking about after-school clubs. (their holidays) 2. When Jody was in Italy, she ate pizza every day. (didn't eat pizza every day) 3. In the holidays, Tina stayed with her uncle and aunt in Cornwall. (grandma and grandad) 4. For the first few days, Tina went surfing every day. (watched a lot of TV and helped on the farm) 5. Mr Barton is Jody and Tina's English teacher. (History)

Tapescript:
(playground noise in the background)

Jody: Hello, Mr Barton.
Mr Barton: Oh, hello, Jody. Hello, Tina. Nice to see you two again. Did you have a good holiday?
Jody and Tina: Yes, thank you, Mr Barton.
Mr Barton: Well, I can see that you had a lot of sun, Jody. You look very brown. Where did you go?
Jody: To Italy.
Mr Barton: Italy, eh? So it was pizza every day, was it?
Jody: No, Mr Barton, not every day. Sometimes we ate spaghetti, too.
Mr Barton: *(laughs)* And what about you, Tina? Did you go away in the holidays?
Tina: Yes, we did. We went down to Cornwall again. My grandma and grandad have got a house there near the sea. So we stayed with them.
Mr Barton: Sounds great. What did you do?
Tina: Well, for the first few days we watched a lot of TV because it rained, and I helped on their farm. But when the sun came out again in the second week, we went surfing, tried abseiling and had a picnic in the fields. That was great!
Mr Barton: Well, it sounds like you enjoyed your holidays. But I guess you're happy to be back at school again.
Tina: Yes, we are, Mr Barton. Are you teaching us in History again this year?
Mr Barton: Um. You're in 8G now, aren't you?
Tina: That's right.
Mr Barton: Well, my timetable tells me that we have a lesson right after break.
Tina: Oh, great.
Mr Barton: OK, girls. See you then. Don't be late.

2 Listening: Big trouble

1. She can't find her planner. 2. She wrote down her Maths homework in it. (She then had P.E. and Music, but they didn't get any homework in these subjects.) 3. Jody has Tina's planner. 4. She found it in her schoolbag.
5. She must put away her books and dirty clothes.

Tapescript:
Mrs Cole: You don't look very happy, Tina. What's up?
Tina: I'm in big trouble, Mum.
Mrs Cole: Why? What's wrong?
Tina: I can't find my planner. You don't know where it is, do you?
Mrs Cole: No, I don't. But don't panic, Tina. Are you sure it isn't in your schoolbag?
Tina: Yes, Mum.
Mrs Cole: Well, where did you have it last?
Tina: That's the problem. I can't remember.
Mrs Cole: Did you have it at school today?
Tina: Um ... Yes, I did. I wrote down my Maths homework in it.
Mrs Cole: OK. So what lessons did you have after Maths?
Tina: Um ... Only P.E. and Music. And we didn't get any homework in those subjects.
Mrs Cole: Hmm ... Did you lose it on your way to P.E.?
Tina: I don't know, Mum. I don't think so.
Mrs Cole: Well, why don't you ask Mr Newman in the morning? Caretakers often find things. Maybe he's got it.
Tina: OK.

(Tina's mobile rings. She answers it.)

Tina: Hi. ... Oh, that's great! Thanks. ... OK. See you in five minutes. *(finishing call and turning to her mum)* That was Jody, Mum. She's got my planner. She found it in her schoolbag. And she's bringing it over now.
Mrs Cole: Good. Then please put those books on the shelf and take your dirty clothes to the bathroom before she gets here.

3 Reading: A special day

Either:
1. right; 2. wrong; 3. wrong; 4. wrong; 5. not in the text; 6. right; 7. not in the text; 8. wrong

Or:
1. She wasn't worried because he is often late. 2. There was a special assembly at school. 3. He came because a girl/another pupil wrote to him and asked for help.
4. They wanted to mutiny against the teachers. 5. They sang pirate songs and Johnny Depp danced to them.
6. He has got a film of Johnny Depp/Captain Jack Sparrow on his mobile.

ISBN: 978-3-12-560016-4

4 Writing: Last Saturday

Lösungsvorschlag:
Last Saturday I woke up at 9 o'clock. First I had breakfast. I had white bread and jam. Then I took Barker to the park. Later I met my friends in town. At 1 o'clock we had lunch together in a snack bar. (The food there is really good/cheap/ nice. / But the food wasn't very good.) In the evening Emma and I went to the sports club. I really enjoyed it. I had a great day. And what did you do? Write soon. Bye. Lisa

5 Writing: Life and school in the past

1. *Lösungsvorschlag:*
In 210 there was no school building or classroom. The teacher met his pupils in a shop in the town centre. The class was really small. The parents paid the teacher. He taught the pupils Latin and Maths. In 210 pupils didn't have books. They wrote on waxed boards and later rubbed out the words or numbers. Most pupils went to school for four years / until they were 12 years old.

2. *Lösungsvorschlag:*
In 1400 school was only for boys from 7 to 14. Often the teachers were priests. The parents didn't pay for lessons, but many families didn't have the money to buy books. So poor people never learnt to read or write. Girls started to work when they were very young.

3. *Lösungsvorschlag:*
In 1885 all children from 5 to 13 went to school. But there were different entrances for boys and girls. They had different classrooms and playgrounds, too. The classes were really big. There were over 60 pupils in one class/ room. They sat behind desks. They repeated what the teachers said. The teachers were very strict.

6 Speaking: Holidays

a) Tina and her parents went/drove to Cornwall./Tina spent her holiday with her parents in Cornwall. They stayed on her grandma and grandad's farm. While they were in Cornwall, they went for a walk and saw lots of sheep. They went to the beach and tried abseiling. One day they went by bike/on a bike tour and had a picnic in the fields. They visited a museum, too. On the last day they put their things in the car and went back home.

b) *individuelle S-Antwort*

7 Speaking: School

Lösungsvorschlag:
A: In Germany children start school when they are six years old. There are about 30 pupils in one class. Boys and girls usually learn together. They don't wear a school uniform. They can wear jeans and T-shirts in school.
In school we don't have assembly. At school we have a library and a computer room. We have a cafeteria, too.
I often eat lunch there. In the afternoon we can go to school clubs, for example basketball, football or choir. At school we mustn't use our mobile phone and we mustn't play ball in the school building.

Lösungsvorschlag:
B: Pupils in Britain must wear a school uniform. They can buy it in the school shop. On Monday morning we always have assembly that's when all the tutor groups meet. We have a computer room, a library and a cafeteria at school. That's where I meet my friends for lunch. In the afternoon we can go to our school clubs. There are many clubs to choose from: water polo, football, tennis, cooking, drama. We have some rules at school. Some of them are: don't play football in the corridors and don't use your mobile phone in lessons.

8 Mediation: At a party

1. Hello, my name is … . And what's your name?
2. Where are you from? 3. Oh, I know Newquay. We spent two weeks there in the summer. 4. Yes, it was great. I liked Newquay. 5. No, we didn't go surfing, but we went swimming in the sea every day. 6. We stayed at a campsite near the beach. 7. Yes, I met a lot of nice people there.
8. I hope you like it here (in Germany).

Extra listening: A phone call to grandma

Diesen Text finden Sie auf der CD-ROM.

Extra reading: Dear Diary

Diesen Text finden Sie auf der CD-ROM.

Green Line 2
Vorschläge zur Leistungsmessung
ISBN: 978-3-12-560016-4

Unit 2 Welcome to London

1 Listening: A day out in London

1. right; 2. wrong; 3. right; 4. right; 5. wrong; 6. right; 7. wrong; 8. right; 9. wrong; 10. right

Tapescript:
(front door opening and closing)
Jody: Hi, Mum. I'm back!
Mrs Cabral: Oh hello, Jody. Did you have a good day out in London?
Jody: Yeah, thanks. Guess who Tina and I met on the DLR?
Mrs Cabral: I've no idea. Who?
Jody: James and his cousin Betty.
Mrs Cabral: I don't think I know Betty. Is she at your school, too?
Jody: No, she isn't. They don't live in Greenwich. But she's nice.
Mrs Cabral: So did you all go shopping together?
Jody: No, we didn't. James and Betty were on their way to London Zoo. They wanted to see the new baby gorilla there.
Mrs Cabral: Hm. Saturday isn't a good day for the zoo. It's usually too full.
Jody: Yes, that's what they told us, too, when we met them again in Oxford Street later. They waited in a queue for two hours and then they saw the gorilla for about five minutes!
Mrs Cabral: So you met them again in Oxford Street?
Jody: Yeah, we had lunch together at a pizza place there.
Mrs Cabral: That's nice. And did you spend the afternoon together, too?
Jody: No. Tina and I wanted to go Harrods after lunch and Betty and James wanted to look around the shops in Oxford Street. But guess who we saw at Bank Station while we were waiting for the DLR?
Mrs Cabral: Your tutor?
Jody: No. Lisa's brother, Ben, and Emma's half-sister, Nasreen.
Mrs Cabral: Are they friends, too?
Jody: Maybe more than friends. They were holding hands and kissing!

2 Listening: A trip to London

1. in her bedroom/upstairs/playing the guitar. 2. with James/her cousin/her aunt and uncle. 3. a house. 4. they didn't have time. 5. a T-shirt for Anna. 6. it is cool/she wants to wear it when she meets with the band.

Tapescript:
Betty: Hello, Mrs Cook. Is Anna at home?
Mrs Cook: Oh, hello, Betty. Yes, she is. She's upstairs in her bedroom. Come in.
Betty: Thank you.
Mrs Cook: You were in London last week, weren't you?
Betty: Yes, we were. We only got back about an hour ago.
Mrs Cook: Did you have a good time?
Betty: Yeah, it was great.
Mrs Cook: Where did you stay?
Betty: With my cousin James. They have a house in Greenwich.
Mrs Cook: Well, from Greenwich you can be in London in no time! That's very useful.
Betty: Yes!
Mrs Cook: And did you visit all the sights?
Betty: Well, not all of them because we didn't have time. But we went to the zoo, had lunch with some of James's friends and went shopping in Oxford Street.
Mrs Cook: Oh, that's nice. But I know that Anna is waiting for you. So just go upstairs.
Betty: Thanks, Mrs Cook.

(Betty goes upstairs. Somebody practising the guitar can be heard. Betty knocks on Anna's door. Anna stops playing the guitar)

Anna: Come in. *(door opening/closing)* Hey, Betty. You're back! *(They kiss Mwaa – Mwaa!)* I didn't hear the door.
Betty: No, you were playing your guitar.
Anna: So how was your trip to London? Did you have a good time?
Betty: Oh, yes, it was great! London was really exciting. Look, I got this for you.
Anna: Hey! A T-shirt! Wow, that's really cool! Thanks. I can wear it this afternoon, when I meet the band.

3 Reading: A trip to the theatre

Either:
(4) When they arrived at the theatre, they sat down in Row 4. (8) Later Mr Jackson told Terry that the man was London's most famous theatre ghost. (7) A moment later, the man was no longer there. (1) Last Saturday Terry and his mother went to the theatre together. (5) At the end of the row, Terry saw a young man. (3) They travelled to Covent Garden by DLR and by Tube. (2) Mr Jackson didn't go with them because he didn't have time. (6) He was wearing funny grey clothes.

Or:
1. They went to the theatre on Saturday (at quarter to twelve). 2. He was busy. / He didn't have time. 3. They got there by DLR and Tube/ Underground. 4. They already had tickets. 5. The sat in Row 4. 6. He was wearing funny grey clothes. / He was wearing a grey cape and a grey hat with three corners. 7. He is London's most famous theatre ghost. 8. Because he always wears grey clothes.

Green Line 2
Vorschläge zur Leistungsmessung
ISBN: 978-3-12-560016-4

4 Writing: A day in London

Individuelle S-Antwort

5 Writing: A photo story

On Saturday Lisa and Ben wanted to do a sightseeing tour of London. First they went to Covent Garden. While they were listening to a busker there, Ben called someone on his mobile phone. After that he gave Lisa his map of London and left. While Lisa was opening the map, a note fell out. It was from 'N'. 'N' wanted to meet Ben at the London Eye at 10.30. Lisa tried to phone Ben, but his mobile was not on. So Lisa and Rob caught the next bus to the London Eye. They saw Ben and Nasreen there. They were holding hands and they were kissing. Later they followed them to Waterloo Station. A train arrived and Ben, Nasreen and Rob got on. But then the doors closed and the train left without Lisa.

6 Speaking: London

a) *Individuelle S-Antwort*

b) Buckingham Palace, Westminster, Hyde Park

c) Madame Tussauds, Tower of London

d) *possible answers:* Buckingham Palace (from outside only); Tower of London (from outside only); Westminster/Big Ben (free); Hyde Park (free)

7 Mediation: A visit to the Natural History Museum

1. Dinosaurier, Blauwal, Riesentintenfisch 2. nichts / der Eintritt ist frei 3. Nein, vom 24. bis 26. Dezember hat es geschlossen. 4. In der Cromwell Road in London./In der Nähe der Haltestelle South Kensington. 5. zu Fuß und mit der U-Bahn oder dem Bus

Extra listening: A phone call

Diesen Text finden Sie auf der CD-ROM.

Extra reading: A thank you letter

Diesen Text finden Sie auf der CD-ROM.

Green Line 2
Vorschläge zur Leistungsmessung
ISBN: 978-3-12-560016-4

Unit 3 Pocket money

1 Listening: Shopping at the supermarket

1. on the kitchen table 2. She thought it was an old list. 3. 9 4. at 7 o'clock 5. *correct answers:* fresh vegetables, fruit, ice-cream, chips, chocolate cakes, bread, drinks, salad, meat 6. ten past five 7. £50.42 8. on the kitchen table

Tapescript:

Mrs Cole: OK, Tina. Let's hurry up! The guests are going to come at seven o'clock for dad's birthday party. Let's see what we need. Where's my list? I always put it in my shopping bag but I can't find it now. That's funny.

Tina: I think it's still on the table in the kitchen, Mum. I saw a list there.

Mrs Cole: Oh, Tina! Why didn't you tell me when we were still at home?

Tina: I thought it was an old list, Mum. I'm sorry.

Mrs Cole: Well, let's try to do the shopping without the list. I think there were nine things on it. Oh, look at the time – it's already half past four: Hm, I know that we need meat, chips and fresh vegetables and salad. There was bread on the list, too. Tina, can you go and get the bread, please? I can get the other things.

Tina: OK, Mum. And don't forget some fruit and ice-cream. Dad always wants ice-cream, but Aunt Mary wants some fruit.

Mrs Cole: OK, Tina! *(talking more to herself)* There's the meat. And here are the fresh vegetables. Where are the salads? Ah, they're over there. We need some drinks too. Oh, and don't forget some chocolate cakes for Grandad Tony. There you are, Tina. Did you get the bread?

Tina: Yes, Mum. What else do we need?

Mrs Cole: Let me think. Hm, I think we have everything. Oh no, it's already ten past five. Let's hurry up and go home.

Assistant at check-out: Good afternoon.

Mrs Cole: Good afternoon.

(scanning of bar codes)

Assistant at check-out: That's £50.42, please.

Mrs Cole: Where's my money? Tina, have you got it?

Tina: No, mum! I think it's on the kitchen table with the list.

Mrs Cole: Oh, no!

2 Listening: Pocket money ideas

Either:

snack bar, cinema, Street Style, mobile

Or:

1. wrong, 2. wrong; 3. right; 4. right; 5. right; 6. wrong James isn't going to go to the cinema with his friends in the evening./Tina and Jody want to meet on Saturday to go shopping./James wants to buy a new mobile phone and top-up cards.

Tapescript:

Tina: James, are you going to come to the cinema with us later? But we're going to eat something first at the Green Village Snack Bar. It's cool there, and the food is cheap.

James: No, sorry. I can't.

Jody: But you're going to come to 'Street Style' with us on Saturday, aren't you? They've got so many cool and stylish clothes! It's great there.

James: I'm sorry, but I can't come. I haven't got much money.

Tina: But you've just got pocket money from your parents, haven't you?

James: That's right, but I want to save it.

Tina: But why, James? Don't you like cool clothes and your friends?

James: Of course I like you and cool clothes and the cinema and … . But I have other ideas. Sorry.

Jody: What do you mean by other ideas? What else do you need? We're your friends. What are you going to do with your pocket money?

James: I want to buy a new mobile phone and top-up cards next week. So I'm going to save my pocket money for that. Then I can text you. That's something for friends, too. And you know, when I watch a DVD at home, it's cheaper than the cinema.

Jody: OK, but then text us when you have pocket money for the next shopping tour. And what about the Green Village snack bar?

James: OK, but just a small hamburger, that isn't too expensive.

Tina: That's great. Let's go to the Green Village Snack Bar and let's have fun.

3 Reading: That's how we spend our pocket money

Either:

1. Jill; 2. Tracy; 3. Julie; 4. Jill & Julie; 5. Julie

Or:

1. d; 2. b, 3. h; 4. a; 5. g; 6. f; 7. e; 8. c

ISBN: 978-3-12-560016-4

4 Writing: More pocket money

Lösungsvorschlag:
Dear Mum and Dad,
I'd like to have some more pocket money, please. Maybe £5 per week, so I can go to the cinema with friends, buy an interesting book or magazine. You always say that reading is so important! I'd like to save some money, too, for our class trip in June. Maybe I can help you and earn some money: I can help Dad to wash the car or in the garden.

5 Writing: Talk to a shop assistant

Lösungsvorschlag:
You: Hello.
SA: Hello. How can I help you?
You: I'm looking for a new mobile phone./I'd like to buy a new mobile phone.
SA: I can show you some. What about this green mobile here?
You: Hm, I'm not sure. I don't like green.
SA: I think we've got it in red, too. Let me see. /Let me just check. Yes, here it is.
You: Oh, that's nice. And how much is it?
SA: That's £32.99.
You: That's OK. Can I have a £5 top-up card, too?
SA: Sure. Here you are.
You: Thank you. Where can I pay?
SA: You can pay over there.
You: Thank you. Goodbye.
SA: Goodbye.

6 Speaking: Money

Individuelle S-Antwort

7 Speaking: Pocket money

Lösungsvorschlag:
Teenager: Mum, I need more pocket money.
Mother: Why do you want more money?
Teenager: I haven't got the money to buy all the things I want.
Mother: Well, what do you want to buy?
Teenager: I want to buy some CDs, a computer game and a cool mobile phone.
Mother: We already give you £30 every month, and that's a lot.
Teenager: But all my friends get more pocket money than I do.
Mother: OK, let's talk to Dad about it when he comes home.

8 Mediation: A role-play

Lösungsvorschlag:
A: Hello, how can I help you?/Are you ready to order?
B: Yes, I'd like a LargeMc, please, and some chips.
A: Small, medium, or large?/Would you like a small, medium or large box of chips?
B: Medium, please. Could I have some ketchup to go with the chips/with my chips?
A: Sure. And would you like a drink?/Anything to drink?
B: No, thanks.
A: That's £3.78.
B: Here you are.
A: Thank you. And that's £1.22 change.
B: Thank you. Goodbye.
A: Goodbye./Bye.

9 Mediation: Shopping for new clothes

Lösungsvorschlag:
1. My friend needs/wants to buy/is looking for a new T-shirt and a (new) pair of jeans. 2. Sie fragt, welche Größe du brauchst und welche Farbe das T-Shirt haben soll. 3. Size M for the jeans and small/size S for the T-shirt. She'd like to have a red T-shirt. 4. Hier sind die Jeans in M und das T-Shirt in S. Sie möchte wissen, ob dir die Farbe gefällt. Du kannst beides anprobieren. 5. She likes the colour. Could you tell us where the changing rooms are? 6. Gleich um die Ecke. 7. The jeans are too expensive. But she'd like to have the T-shirt. Where can she pay (for it)? 8. Du kannst da drüben zahlen.

Extra listening: At Street Style

Diesen Text finden Sie auf der CD-ROM.

Extra reading: Souvenirs of London

Diesen Text finden Sie auf der CD-ROM.

Green Line 2
Vorschläge zur Leistungsmessung
ISBN: 978-3-12-560016-4

Unit 4 Who wants to be a star?

1 Listening: Robbie Williams

Either:

1. wrong; 2. wrong; 3. right; 4. wrong; 5. right; 6. right; 7. wrong; 8. right; 9. wrong; 10. wrong

Or:

1. Stoke-on-Trent, Staffordshire 2. his mum and his sister 3. sing and do tricks and perform them for other people 4. not good at school, told a lot of jokes, always liked to perform and sing, always wanted to become a star 5. at an audition 6. he was tired and they had a lot of problems in the band 7. in February 1996 8. fifteen years later

Tapescript:

DJ Rick: As we've already told you, Robbie is ill. So, his manager is with us. Thank you for coming.

Manager: Thank you.

DJ Rick: Robbie was born in Stoke-on-Trent, Staffordshire, is that right?

Manager: Yes, he lived with his mum and his sister Sally. His father left the family.

DJ Rick: How old was he when that happened?

Manager: He was three. But even before that his dad, Peter, wasn't at home very often. They saw him sometimes. His dad liked to sing and do tricks and perform them for other people. When he was at home, he and Robbie's mum had fights and he left very often. Still, Robbie liked his dad's skills, but he doesn't know much about him and what he's doing now.

DJ Rick: OK. You know, we have a lot of young listeners. What can you tell us about Robbie's schooldays?

Manager: Well, he wasn't good at school. He made a lot of jokes and the teachers didn't like that. But he really liked performing and singing and he always wanted to become a star.

DJ Rick: So when did it all start then?

Manager: Um, Robbie worked for BBC Radio Stoke to get some money. And one day his mum saw in the newspaper that they were looking for boys for a new pop group. This was back in 1990. They wanted boys between 15 and 17, so he was the right one. *(sounding pleased)*

DJ Rick: That was the start of the band Take That?

Manager: Yes, it was. He met the other four boys at the audition. They became famous and had a lot of fun together.

DJ Rick: But why did Robbie leave the band in 1995?

Manager: Well, he was tired and they had a lot of problems in the band – it was too much.

DJ Rick: So when was the end of Take That?

Manager: That was in 1996, in February.

DJ Rick: I remember all the fans that were crying.

Manager: Of course, they were very sad. But the band was tired and it was time to stop. But now, fifteen years later *(proudly announcing)* they are back again. They like the fans and they enjoy being back.

DJ Rick: Robbie must be very happy. And now he's married, too. Congratulations!

Manager: *(enthusiastic)* Yes, it's great.

DJ Rick: Thank you for taking the time for the interview. And we wish the band good luck. Now let's listen to their latest song … *(fade out)*

2 Listening: Stars and their prizes

	won a prize yet?	plans to win another prize?	if not, why?
football player	yes	yes	/
singer	yes	no	became too much; fell ill; is taking a break
actor	no	yes	still young, many good actors
model	yes	no	school, friends and family are more important

Tapescript:

Football player: Oh! What a question? Of course I've already won a lot of championships with my team: We've already won two League Cups.
We were successful and we still want to be successful football players. We're all one team and we can only win together, you see. We want more national and international titles.

Singer: Oh yes, I've already won two music prizes. When I was at school, I won first place at a music talent show. Then I won a national competition. And it became too much for me. I lost a lot of friends. I was nervous and I couldn't perform for a large group of people any more. I couldn't eat anything and I fell ill. Now I'm taking a break. I don't work to win more prizes. It's better that way.

Actor: No, I haven't won any prizes yet, but I'm still young. I really like to act. I'd like to win an Oscar one day. But life in Hollywood is hard. There are just so many good actors. You need a lot of luck in this job.

Model: Oh yes, I won Next Top Model and I made a lot of money. And I met beautiful supermodel Elle Macpherson – that was great. I'm in my last year of school, so at the moment I'm very busy with my school subjects. I haven't got much time for new competitions. I don't want to forget my friends and my family.

Green Line 2
Vorschläge zur Leistungsmessung
ISBN: 978-3-12-560016-4

3 Reading: Britain's Got Talent

Either:

1. sing, dance, do sports; 2. at home; in the studio; 3. gets some money, can show his/her skills in front of the Royal Family; 4. in different British cities; 5. People that phone from home choose; 6. normal people with talent can become famous

Or:

good	not so good
- win money - normal people can become famous - perform in front of the Royal Family - you can see people with different skills - auditions take place in different towns/people don't have to travel far	- they show people with no/little talent, too - people didn't get any food or anything to drink while they were waiting to audition

4 Writing: My favourite ...

Individuelle S-Antwort

5 Writing: An audition

Individuelle S-Antwort

Hi Lisa,
Guess what! I'm going to go to an audition next week. I read about it in my favourite magazine. I've already practised the song a thousand times. I've found some cool clothes and I've dyed my hair, too. But I don't know how to dance to the song. I haven't had an idea yet. You're a good dancer. Can you help me?
I'd really want to go to the audition and win because the three best singers can meet their favourite star.
Bye. Laura

6 Speaking: Would you like to be a star?

Individuelle S-Antwort

7 Mediation: Stars

Lösungsvorschlag:

I: Hello. It's nice to have you here.
S: Thank you. It's nice to be here.
I: I went to your concert. It was great! Are you nervous before you go on stage?
S: Well, yes, sometimes when I play in front of lots of people/fans.
I: Do you do anything special before you go on stage? / Is there anything special you do before you go on stage?
S: I always put a penny in my trouser pocket.
I: Oh, that's interesting. And tell me, how did it all start?
S: Well, I put some of my own songs on the Internet.
I: And five years later you're famous. Do you like it/to be a star?
S: It's great! But there's little/isn't much time for my friends and family. I'm not often at home. I'm often on TV or give interviews. It's hard to find time to sit down and write new songs and to practise them. But I've always wanted to become a star.
I: Well, it was nice to talk to you. Thank you very much for the interview. Good luck. / And good luck to you.
S: Thank you. Bye.

8 Mediation: Teen Buzz Magazine

Lösungsvorschlag:

Im *Teen Buzz Magazine* suchen sie nach Sängern zwischen 10 und 16.
Die Zeitschrift selbst.
Am 3. März. Das ist ein Montag.
Man muss eine gute Stimme haben, seine eigenen Klamotten und ein paar seiner Fans mitbringen. (Und sich selbst natürlich.)
Im Jugendzentrum in Greenwich.
Für eine Musikshow.
Die besten Drei gewinnen ein Treffen mit ihrem Lieblingsstar und können ihren Song aufnehmen.

Extra listening: An audition
Diesen Text finden Sie auf der CD-ROM.

Extra reading: 'Schweini', our football star
Diesen Text finden Sie auf der CD-ROM.

Green Line 2
Vorschläge zur Leistungsmessung
ISBN: 978-3-12-560016-4

Unit 5 Fit for life

1 Listening: Is it the same everywhere?

Either:

a) James: football, basketball, orienteering, canoeing, skating; Yannik: climbing
b) James: orienteering; Yannik: climbing

Or:

1. eggs and bacon 2. after school 3. map, compass 4. run fast, read maps well 5. school, sports/climbing club 6. too much homework

Tapescript:

Yannik: Mm. I like these cornflakes. Do you always have cornflakes? We learnt that people in England always have eggs and bacon for breakfast.
James: *(laughing)* Ah, well, you shouldn't believe everything you learn at school. We never have eggs and bacon. *(short pause)* Yannik, I'm going to orienteering club after school today. Do you want to come?
Yannik: Orienteering? What's that?
James: It's great. You have to run from one place to another as fast as you can and …
Yannik: *(interrupting)* Oh, we run in our sports lessons, too. I don't like that.
James: No, but this is better. You don't just run around a field. You need a compass. The teacher or somebody gives you a map and you must find some places on the map and finish first.
Yannik: Oh, that sounds fun. Must you run the whole time?
James: No, but people who are good at orienteering can read maps well and run fast, too.
Yannik: Do lots of people do it? I've never heard of it before.
James: Well, it's very popular at our school, but you can't do it at all schools.
Yannik: What other sports can you do at your school?
James: Oh, er … football, basketball … and we have a skating club, too. What sports do you do at your school?
Yannik: We can only do sports in our sports lessons. If we want to do other sports or join a team, we must join a club. I'm in a climbing club and …
James: Rock climbing?
Yannik: Yeah.
James: Oh, that sounds good. Do you go climbing in the mountains?
Yannik: Yes, we sometimes go away for a weekend and climb in the mountains. And we practise on a climbing wall every week.
James: Oh, I'd like to try that.
Yannik: You can come with me when you visit me in Germany. Isn't there a climbing club near here?
James: I don't know. I don't really have much time to go climbing. In the summer I'm going to join the water sports club. I'd like to learn to row and I'd really like to try a canoe on the river.
Yannik: Oh, I'd like to do that, too. There's never enough time, is there?
James: No, it's because we get too much homework.
Yannik: Yes, some things are the same everywhere.

2 Listening: At the hospital

a) arm, hand, toe

b) arm, basketball, headache, sick, hospital, pushed the door, tests

Tapescript:

Doctor: Can I look at your arm now?
Tina: Ow!
Doctor: Can you move your hand?

(short pause)

Doctor: Hm. That looks broken. We'll check that. And what about your head? Does it hurt when you move it?
Tina: No.
Doctor: Do you have a headache? Or feel sick?
Tina: I don't have a headache but I feel a little sick.
Doctor: That may be the shock. What happened?
Tina: Well, I was playing basketball at school and Jody threw the ball to me. She threw it hard and so I ran fast. Somebody from the other team – I don't know who it was – ran in front of me and I fell over her foot. I don't think she did it deliberately.
Doctor: And did you hit your arm and head on the floor[1]?
Tina: Yeah, but it didn't hurt very much at first, but then the trainer thought my arm looked funny and called my parents right away.
Doctor: Well, they were right to bring you to hospital. Does anything else[2] hurt?
Tina: Yes, my big toe.
Doctor: Oh, did you hurt that when you fell, too?
Tina: No, I hurt it when I was walking into the hospital. I wanted to open the door but a man was coming the other way. I didn't see him and he didn't see me. He was walking really fast and when he pushed the door, it hit my toe.
Doctor: Oh no. You haven't been very lucky today.
Tina: Well, it hasn't all been bad.
Doctor: Oh? Did something good happen, too?
Tina: Well, we've got three tests this week and now I can't do them, can I?

[1]floor – *(Fuß-)Boden*; [2]else – *sonst noch, noch was*

3 Reading: Young sportsperson of the year

a) 1. wrong, 2. right, 3. right, 4. right, 5. wrong, 6. right

b) 1. Nick/He is one of the best horseback-riders in Britain. 5. His mum/She says that he needs time to meet his friends and just chill.

4 Writing: An accident

Lösungsvorschlag:
On Saturday at about 11 o'clock two boys were playing football in the garden, when a boy rode his bike down the hill. He was near the boys when they kicked the ball onto the street. The boy on the bike couldn't stop and so the ball hit the bike. The boy fell off his bike and onto the road. His head was bleeding. Then his dad/a man came and helped him to get up. He took the boy to hospital.

5 Writing: Family pictures

Lösungsvorschlag:
Molly started to play tennis when she was very young. She tried to hit the tennis balls in her parents' garden. Later she practised regularly with a trainer/her dad on the tennis court. Molly tries to keep fit. She often goes jogging. She has a training plan. She trains four times/days per week. But still she finds time to meet her friends and go to the cinema.

6 Speaking: How do you keep fit?

a) *Lösungsvorschlag:*
Many teenagers in Britain do sports. The most popular sport is swimming. Teenagers like to ride their bikes, to play football or tennis, too.
But teenagers don't eat a lot of healthy food. They like white bread, chips, sweets and soft drinks. Fruits and vegetables are not so popular.

b) *Lösungsvorschlag:*
Every morning I get up and wash my hands and my face. I brush/clean/do my teeth, too. Then I have breakfast. I usually have some bread and some fruit. I usually sleep about/for 9 hours at night. I don't smoke. My parents/teachers say that you mustn't smoke because it's bad for your health. I do sports at school and every Tuesday I go to football club. Sometimes I go on a bike tour with my parents at the weekend. My mum takes me to the doctor's regularly.

7 Speaking: £150 to spend

Lösungsvorschlag:
A: We have £150. What can we do with the money?
B: We can buy some new footballs.
A: We already have a lot of footballs at our school. How about a few exciting books? Real adventure stories would be nice.
B: I'm not sure. Have you ever been to the school library? There are lots and lots of books there.
A: Maybe we could have a party with our class or go on a trip together.
B: I'm sure it's expensive, and we are a large class.
A: I know – we can paint our classroom.
B: That's a good idea. I'm sure that will be fun!

8 Mediation: A holiday in the Black Forest

You can go climbing, horse riding, canoeing, swimming and go for walks.
They've got good/great teachers for all sports/activities.
It's OK if you have the right equipment and the right clothes. The teachers will explain everything to you. But still you need to be careful.
Yes, you need good shoes/hiking boots, warm clothes and an anorak.
In a house. It's in the (heart of the) Black Forest. There are six bedrooms. Every bedroom has 10 beds.

Extra listening: Stop that!

Diesen Text finden Sie auf der CD-ROM.

Extra reading: An interview

Diesen Text finden Sie auf der CD-ROM.

Green Line 2
Vorschläge zur Leistungsmessung
ISBN: 978-3-12-560016-4

Unit 6 In Scotland

1 Listening: A weekend in Scotland

Either:

1. right; 2. right; 3. wrong; 4. wrong; 5. right; 6. wrong; 7. right; 8. right

Or:

1. Jody, Aaron, Bruno, mum 2. visit mum's friends
3. climb Ben Nevis, have a picnic, visit Loch Ness, watch a football match 4. James is worried because Aaron fell and hurt his arm. They've got a football match on Saturday.
5. it's scared of tourists, it's a story/there is no monster

Tapescript:

Tina: Hi Jody, did you have a good weekend? You were in Scotland, weren't you?
Jody: Yeah, we visited my mum's friends. It was great!
James: And what about your brother? Did he like it, too?
Jody: Well, it was boring for Aaron at first. He didn't have his computer or anyone to play with.
Tina: So did you do anything exciting while you were there?
Jody: Well, on the first day we drove all the way to Fort William and climbed Ben Nevis. Bruno loved the hills! But when we got to the top he was tired because of all the rocks.
Tina: Oh, and I guess you had a picnic.
Jody: *(laughs)* Yeah, picnics are a real must in our family.
James: And what else did you do?
Jody: On Saturday we visited Loch Ness. Aaron wanted to see Nessie. And while he was running around, he fell because the rocks were wet.
James: Oh, no! We've got an important football match on Saturday. He didn't get hurt, did he?
Jody: Well, he hurt his arm. But I'm sure he'll be OK on Saturday. Oh, and my mum had a special surprise for Aaron.
James: Like what?
Jody: She had tickets for a football match in Inverness.
James: Lucky him. Who did they play?
Jody: Hm, let me think … . Oh, I remember now, Inverness Caledonian Thistle Football Club played Celtic Glasgow.
James: Ohhh, Celtic is one of my favourite teams!
Tina: And what about Nessie? Did you see the monster?
Jody: No. It never came out of the water. Maybe it was scared because of all the tourists there.
James: Or maybe because it's just a story?

2 Listening: Weekend plans

Tina: shopping with mum; visit grandma; homework (English, Maths, Biology)
Jody: homework (English, Maths, Biology); aunt, uncle and cousin come to visit; have a picnic; play with Eric/cousin
Aaron: watch the football match

Tapescript:

Jody: Hey Tina, how did you like our English lesson today?
Tina: I don't know. Mrs Green wasn't very friendly today: That was a lot of homework we got from her! And there's still a lot to do for Maths and Biology at the weekend.
Jody: Oh, I forgot about Maths and Biology. Thanks for reminding me. That's going to be a lot of work! Do you have any other plans for the weekend?
Tina: Yes, my mum and I are going to have a look at the shops in Greenwich. Mum wants to buy a new skirt and new T-shirts for me. My old ones are going to be too small this summer.
Jody: Great. That will be fun! What else are you going to do?
Tina: On Sunday afternoon we're going to visit grandma. She's been ill for two weeks now. But what about your plans?
Jody: My aunt and uncle and my little cousin Eric are going to visit us.
Tina: How old is Eric?
Jody: He's five and really sweet. But what can I do with him all day long? He'll need someone to play with while our parents drink tea and talk. If the weather is nice, we'll all go to Greenwich Park and have a picnic together. He can run around and we can play ball.
Tina: Oh, that's nice. Did you know that England is playing Scotland on Saturday?
Jody: No, I didn't. Maybe Eric can watch the match with Aaron. I'm sure he'll want to watch the game.
Tina: Listen, I have to go. I'll see you on Monday.
Jody: Yes, see you on Monday. Bye.

3 Reading: The Battle of Bannockburn

1. he knows a lot about Scottish history and it's very interesting. 2. he thinks that the Scottish army won't be a problem. He is not interested in Scotland. 3. a soldier tries/tried to kill 4. – the Earls didn't work together as a team, – the English weren't fast enough, – the Scots believed they could win

Green Line 2
Vorschläge zur Leistungsmessung
ISBN: 978-3-12-560016-4

4 Writing: An exchange

Lösungsvorschlag:

Hello,

Thanks for your e-mail. In your e-mail you asked us what we would like to see and do while we're in Scotland.

We'd like to visit Edinburgh and the castle because we've heard a lot about it in school. We'd love to see some of the Scottish hills and mountains, too. Maybe we can climb Ben Nevis. On our way there we'd like to stop at Loch Ness. As nobody has ever seen the monster, we'd like to be the first to find it.

We can't wait to see you! Bye, ...

5 Writing: A story

Lösungsvorschlag:

- Laura is too scared and won't go with the boys.
- The boys will go alone. They will find the ghost. The ghost will fight with/against the boys. They will get hurt and call/shout for help.
- Laura will come and help them.

6 Speaking: Plans

Lösungsvorschlag:

A: Saturday will be a nice day. Let's climb Ben Nevis on Saturday.

B: No, we can't climb Ben Nevis on Saturday. The tour is every Friday and Monday.

A: Hm, well, it will be raining/will rain on Friday. So let's go on Monday.

B: Yes. But what can we do on Friday?

A: Let's see. We can go to Loch Ness, go on a guided tour around Edinburgh or go to a bagpipes concert.

B: Loch Ness isn't a good idea in bad weather. Let's sleep late and then go on the guided tour.

A: Which one? There's a tour at 1 o'clock and at 3 o'clock.

B: Hm, let's go on the 1 o'clock tour.

A: Good idea, and in the evening we can go to the bagpipes concert.

B: Yes, let's do that. But what about Saturday?

A: Well, we can just walk around Edinburgh or sit in a café.

B: And we can visit the museum in the castle.

A: That sounds good.

B: And on Sunday we can go to Loch Ness.

A: Yes, it'll be nice and sunny then.

7 Speaking: A tourist guide

Lösungsvorschlag:

Edinburgh Castle is the most famous/popular place in Edinburgh. It's on a hill called Castle Rock. The castle is over 1,000 years old. Every year in August the Military Tattoo takes place in front of the castle, where we're standing now. There are bagpipe bands and there's a lot of dancing going on. About 200,000 visitors come to the festival every year.

There's one more interesting thing I'd like to tell you. Every day at 1 o'clock you can hear the 'One o'clock gun', so people can check their watch. In the old days you could hear the gun even if you were three kilometres away. That means the gun could tell the captain of a ship what time it was and that they were near Edinburgh/the coast.

8 Speaking: A holiday picture

Lösungsvorschlag:

I took this picture when we visited Edinburgh Castle. We saw the Military Tattoo. There were a lot of people. You can see the Scots in their Scottish dress in the picture. They're wearing kilts. They're dancing and playing the bagpipes.

9 Mediation: At the post office

Excuse me, my grandma wants/would like to write some postcards to her friends. She needs some stamps./Do you have any stamps?

Sie fragt, wo deine Freunde wohnen und ob du schon Karten hast. Sie haben nämlich welche dort drüben.

They live in Germany. She's already got the postcards.

Sie fragt, ob du normale oder besondere Briefmarken (Sondermarken) willst.

What are special stamps?

Die Sondermarken sind schöner und etwas teurer. Einige sammeln sie.

The normal ones will do./She'll have the normal ones./She'd like the normal ones. How much are they? Where can we find a letter box?

Eine kostet 60 Pence. Das macht zusammen £2,40. Der Briefkasten ist draußen rechts vorm Gebäude.

How long will the cards take?

Etwa eine Woche.

Thank you for your help.

Extra listening: Clichés

Diesen Text finden Sie auf der CD-ROM.

Extra reading: How Arthur got Excalibur

Diesen Text finden Sie auf der CD-ROM.

Green Line 2
Vorschläge zur Leistungsmessung
ISBN: 978-3-12-560016-4

Unit 7 English everywhere

1 Listening: Going abroad

1. Paris; 2. 8.25; 3. AF 8956; 4. Charles de Gaulle Airport; 5. you should always keep your bags with you and tell someone if you see a bag without its owner; 6. Mr Allister is late for his flight; 7. C 89; 8. B 27, 28, 29

Tapescript:

Tina: Mum, when does our flight to Paris leave?

Mrs Cole: It leaves at 8.25 and we'll arrive at 10.40. So we can start sightseeing in the afternoon.

Tina: So the flight takes over two hours.

Mrs Cole: No, darling. There's a one-hour time difference[1].

Mr Cole: I'm so excited! I haven't been to Paris for 15 years and I'm sure it's changed a lot!

Mrs Cole: Yes, I think so, too. I'm sure it looks very different now. But Bob, have you already found out which check-in desk we need to go to?

Mr Cole: No, not yet. I didn't see it on the information board when we came in. Tina, have you seen where our check-in is?

Tina: No, sorry dad, but there's an information board over there. Let's go and find out.

Mr Cole: What's our flight number again?

Mrs Cole: That's AF 8956.

Mr Cole: Hm, oh, there it is. It says AF 8956 to Paris Charles de Gaulle. The flight is on time. Check-in starts in five minutes and the check-in desks are 23–28. They should be over there, shouldn't they?

Mrs Cole: Yes, you're right.

Tina: Good, let's go then!

Airport announcement: All passengers should make sure that they have their baggage and other personal things with them at all times. Don't leave your baggage unattended[2]. If you see any unattended baggage, please tell the security officers[3]. Don't touch[4] unattended baggage and never open it.

Tina: What did he say mum? I couldn't understand him. It's so loud and busy here!

Mrs Cole: He said that you should always have your baggage with you. And if you find a bag without its owner, you should tell the people that work here. You mustn't go near the bag or open it.

Tina: Why?

Mr Cole: Because you don't know what people carry in their bags. Maybe it's something that can hurt you.

Mrs Cole: Look, there's our check-in desk. And they've just started with the check-in.

Airport announcement: Last call for Mister Allister. Mister Allister, please come to gate[5] H78 quickly. Your flight to New York is ready for takeoff. Mister Allister, please come to gate H78.

Mr Cole: Tina, did you understand the name? Was the announcement for us?

Tina: No, dad! It was for someone called Allister. Don't worry, we're OK.

Stewardess: Good morning! May I have your passports and tickets, please?

Mr Cole: Here you are.

Stewardess: OK. Your seats[6] are B 27, 28 and 29 and your gate is C89. Enjoy your flight.

Mr Cole: Thank you very much.

Stewardess: You're welcome.

[1]difference – *Unterschied;* [2]unattended – *unbeaufsichtigt;* [3]security officer – *Sicherheitspersonal;* [4]touch – *anfassen;* [5]gate – *Ausgang/ Flugsteig;* [6]seat – *Platz*

2 Listening: At the travel agent's

Germany; tours/ones; six; twelve; 12-day/longer; Hamburg; guide; Berlin; Dresden; mountains; surprise; finishes/ends; chocolate museum; souvenirs; July the 2nd; the 13th; hotels; breakfast

Tapescript:

Travel Agent: Good morning! How can I help you?

Mrs Green: Good morning. I'd like to go away for a few days. Maybe Germany. They have a lot of nice and interesting places, haven't they? Are there any tours?

TA: Yes, of course. Have a seat, please. Let me see ... Hm, we've got two different tours. The first tour is 6 days and starts in Berlin. It then goes on to Munich and Cologne.

Mrs Green: Hm, six days isn't very long. You don't get much time to see the sights. What about the other tour?

TA: Well, the other one is twelve days. It starts in Hamburg.

Mrs Green: Oh, I hear it's a nice town.

TA: Yes, it's beautiful. A guide there will show you the city and tell you about its history. He'll take you to the harbour and the "Speicherstadt", too, which is very interesting.

Mrs Green: And how many days is that?

TA: You've got two nights there. And then you go on to Berlin.

Mrs Green: That's great. I've always wanted to go to Berlin. Do we get a tour there, too?

Green Line 2
Vorschläge zur Leistungsmessung
ISBN: 978-3-12-560016-4

TA: Well, in the brochure it says "boat tour on the River Spree", and then you'll visit the museum island, the Brandenburg Gate[1] and the Reichstag.
Mrs Green: Um, that's a lot.
TA: But you've got three days there.
Mrs Green: That's OK, then. What's the next stop?
TA: It's Dresden.
Mrs Green: Oh, that's where the famous theatre is, isn't it?
TA: Yes, and you'll go there in the evening.
Mrs Green: What else is there to see?
TA: It's got a famous church, the Frauenkirche, and a few museums. There's a castle near the town which you can go to by boat.
Mrs Green: So that's two nights in Dresden, I guess.
TA: Yes, and then you go to Munich. There you'll have a guided tour and see the Liebfrauendom and the new stadium[2].
Mrs Green: Oh, my husband[3] will love that.
TA: If he's interested in going to a football match, I can try to book tickets for you, but they'll cost extra.
Mrs Green: Let's do that. That will be a nice surprise.
TA: OK, but let me finish the tour first. Munich is close to the mountains so you'll have a day to go on a mountain hike and to visit one of the beautiful lakes.
Mrs Green: That's nice to spend some time outside the city.
TA: Yes, and your last stop is two days in Cologne. There you can visit the chocolate museum, the big church, the River Rhine or go shopping and buy some souvenirs. How does that sound to you?
Mrs Green: Lovely. And could you tell me the dates and how we get to Germany?
TA: The tour starts on July the 2nd and you'll be back in London on the 13th. You'll fly from London Heathrow to Hamburg, and then on the way back you'll fly out of Cologne.
Mrs Green: And the hotel situation?
TA: All the hotels are nice and have wonderful big breakfasts.
Mrs Green: Great! Can you book the tour for me and my husband, please?
TA: Well of course. I just need your names and address … *(fading you)*

[1]Gate – *Tor*; [2]stadium – *Stadion*; [3]husband – *Ehemann*

3 Reading: Heathrow Airport and the Channel Tunnel

1. She chose Heathrow Airport and the Channel Tunnel as part of a project about London transport and because the holidays are near and many people are going to go abroad. She thinks that Londoners use the airport and the tunnel, but don't know much about them. 2. She got the information from books and the Internet. 3. It's in Hillingdon just outside London. 4. They can get there by bus, taxi, car, bike, train or Underground. 5. No, it isn't. (It's the second busiest airport.) 6. There are five terminals and two runways. 7. They look after the buildings, work in shops and restaurants and help when there is a fire. 8. Heathrow Airport 9. It took six years to build it. (1988–1994) 10. People first talked about it about 200 years ago, but they didn't know how to build it. 11. Yes, the Queen. 12. The tunnel is 37.9 km long and 100 m underwater. 13. No, it isn't. (It's the second longest after the Seikan Tunnel.) 14. 300 km/h 15. 2 hours and 20 minutes.

4 Writing: Visit Britain

Lösungsvorschlag:
The Channel Tunnel
The tunnel links Great Britain and France. So there are two terminals – one is on the French coast and the other one on the British coast.
The tunnel is 37.9 km long and about 100 m underwater. Two trains can travel through the tunnel. There is a smaller tunnel, too, so people can leave the tunnel if the train breaks down or if there is a fire.

Heathrow Airport
Heathrow Airport is in Hillingdon, just outside London. You can get there by train or Underground. The airport has got five terminals and two runways. It has shops, restaurants and a hotel, too.

5 Writing: Holidays

Individuelle S-Antwort

6 Writing: My tips

Individuelle S-Antwort

7 Speaking: A visit to the UK

Individuelle S-Antwort

Green Line 2
Vorschläge zur Leistungsmessung
ISBN: 978-3-12-560016-4

8 Mediation: On the plane

Lösungsvorschlag:

Sie sagt, dass man während des Fluges angeschnallt und sitzen bleiben soll. Die Rettungsweste befindet sich unter dem Sitz. Bei Fragen soll man sich an sie wenden.
She'd like a glass of water, please.
Sie sagt, dass gleich Wasser, Tee und Kaffee für alle Passagiere serviert wird.
Wollen Sie Kaffee, Tee oder Wasser?
She'd like a cup of tea and a glass of water. Do you have any German magazines?
Sie fragt, ob Sie sonst noch etwas brauchen.
No thanks. Not now.

Extra listening: At the reception

Diesen Text finden Sie auf der CD-ROM.

Extra Reading: Sam's story

Diesen Text finden Sie auf der CD-ROM.

ISBN: 978-3-12-560016-4

Unit 1 Back to school

1 Wordwise: School words

1. assembly; 2. timetable; 3. subject; 4. lesson(s); 5. break; 6. uniform

2 Wordwise: Mixed bag

school; enjoy; were; almost; stopped; Then; ate; please; didn't; parents; stayed; built; afternoon; rode; went; saw; scary; What; played; too

3 Language: Rob's first day at TTS

was; wore; arrived; met; said; smiled; started; took; asked; told; laughed; were; went; bought; sat; collected; looked

4 Language: Lots of questions

1. Did; Yes, he did. 2. Was; No, it wasn't. 3. Were; No, there weren't. 4. Did; No, she didn't. 5. Did; No, they didn't. 6. Were; No, I wasn't. / Yes, I was.

5 Language: The first day

1. What time/When did morning tutorial start? 2. Where did Lisa and Rob play football at break? 3. What did Rob eat for lunch? 4. How many lessons were there before morning break? 5. When did Rob do his homework? 6. Why did he go to bed early? 7. Who was very happy?

6 Language: But …

2. He didn't go to school by bike. He went to school by car. 3. The first lesson wasn't German. It was Technology. 4. Rob didn't have lunch in the classroom. He had lunch in the cafeteria. 5. School didn't finish after the last lesson. It finished after afternoon tutorial.

7 Language: The weekend

Did you have; had; played; went; took; was; Did you see; didn't see; were; didn't want; saw; were; rode; was; stopped; survived; enjoyed; Did you find; Was it; told; did

Unit 2 Welcome to London

1 Wordwise: Words

2. escalator/two escalators; pidgeon/two pigeons; a queue; the Tube/Underground/train; six passengers

2 Wordwise: Opposites

2. to leave; 3. to get on; 4. to cry; 5. worse than; 6. the shortest; 7. warmer than; 8. the most expensive

3 Language: one and ones

1. a black one and a blue one; 2. two big/large ones and a small one; 3. an old one and a new one; 4. The one with (the) red hair.

4 Language: have got and have

a) 2. don't have; 3. doesn't have; 4. didn't have; 5. aren't having; hasn't got.

b) 1. Where have they got a small flat?/Where do they have a small flat? 2. How many bedrooms has it got?/ How many bedrooms does it have? 3. What does Emma's dad have?/What has Emma's dad got? 4. When did they have a house in Bristol?

5 Language: An unlucky day for some

1. were sitting; stopped; fell 2. hurt; was getting; caught 3. lost; was running 4. was waiting; saw, were holding; were kissing/kissed 5. was crossing; came, ran

6 Language: Can we go to Hamleys?

good; big/large; the most famous; the oldest; the most popular; terrible; better; nice; aren't/not as expensive as; boring; more exciting; more scary; bigger/larger than; bad; full

Green Line 2
Vorschläge zur Leistungsmessung
ISBN: 978-3-12-560016-4

Unit 3 Pocket money

1 Wordwise: A menu

1. fish and chips 2. salad 3. chicken/meat 4. pizza 5. fresh vegetables 6. burger/hamburger

2 Wordwise: Shopping

1. shopping; 2. money; 3. assistants; 4. clothes; 5. changing

3 Language: Question tags

a) doesn't it; do you; weren't they
b) isn't it; weren't they; didn't you; can you

4 Language: 's or s'

1. Lisa's; 2. Our friends'; 3. My friend's; 4. The girls'; 5. Tracy's; 6. Mr Colin's; 7. people's; 8. women's

5 Language: What are they going to do?

2. Lisa and Emma are going to buy (new) trainers. 3. Karen is going to answer Bob's text message. / Karen is going to answer the text message. Karen is going to answer her friend. 4. The friends are going to eat pizza. 5. Mrs Taylor is going to listen to music. 6. Mr Taylor is going to wash the/his car.

6 Language: The weekend

a) 1. Are you going to visit your grandma and grandad? – Yes, I am./Yes, I'm going to visit my grandma and grandad. 2. Are you going to do your homework? – Yes, I am./Yes, I'm going to do my homework. 3. Are you going to go to the cinema? – No, I'm not. / No, I'm not going to go to the cinema. 4. Are you going to play computer games? – Yes, I am./ Yes, I'm going to play computer games.

b) 1. Did you help your mum in the kitchen? – Yes, I did./ Yes, I helped my mum in the kitchen.
2. Did you watch TV? – Yes, I did./Yes, I did watch TV.
3. Did you write an e-mail? – Yes, I did./Yes, I did write an e-mail.
4. Did you spend your/any money on sweets? – No, I didn't./No, I didn't spend my/any money on sweets.

7 Language: The shopping list

some; anything; any; some; any; Somebody/ Someone; something; some; somewhere

Unit 4 Who wants to be a star?

1 Wordwise: Who wants to be a star?

1. practise; 2. audition; 3. stage; 4. good-looking; 5. drummers; 6. tour; 7. radio; 8. money

2 Wordwise: Past participles

taken, fallen, had; found; said; become; lost; talked; left; learnt/learned; won; got/gotten; done; sung; seen; checked; met; bought; sold; written; woken up

3 Language: What have they done?

2. Lisa and Jade have just built a sand castle.
3. The children have just written invitation cards.
4. Terry has just woken up. 5. Tiger has just jumped through the window. 6. Tom has just done his homework.

4 Language: Have you ever ...?

Have you ever been to London?
Have you ever played basketball?
Have you ever helped your dad in the garden?
Have you ever been/gone shopping with your mum?
Have you ever invited all your friends to your house?
Have you ever sung a song in front of lots of people?
Have you ever had a pet?
Have you ever lost your money?

5 Language: just or not yet

The bus has just left.
The train hasn't gone yet.
She hasn't gone out yet.
He hasn't opened his/the present yet.
They haven't finished their homework yet.
It has just stopped raining.

6 Language: Simple past or present perfect

Have you ever spoken; met; have you ever been; went; Did you have; enjoyed; Have you seen; went; haven't seen; Have you ever had; had; thought; was

ISBN: 978-3-12-560016-4

Unit 5 Fit for life

1 Wordwise: Sports

Sports: rock climbing, aerobics, orienteering, judo
Equipment: life-jacket, anorak, canoe
People: trainer, swimmer, reporter

2 Wordwise: Body parts

Abbildung Turner: head, mouth, neck, arm, leg, toe
Abbildung Fußballerin: eye, nose, finger, shoulder, stomach, knee, foot

3 Wordwise: Adjectives

overweight, embarrassing, angry, friendly, healthy, hard, careful, heavy

4 Language: An interview

a) 1. Where do you come from? 2. Who taught you judo? 3. Who trains with you? 4. What do you think about … 5. What makes you feel happier – your friends or judo?
b) *Lösungsvorschlag:*
Who/What helps you to keep fit? / What's more important for you – school or going swimming? / What makes you feel happy / angry? / What's your favourite food?

5 Language: School reports

1. in a friendly way, hard, carefully 2. quietly, nervously, well 3. beautifully, fast

6 Language: My family

1. the fastest 2. harder, the hardest 3. worse, the worst 4. better, the best 5. better/more beautiful, the best/the most beautiful

Unit 6 In Scotland

1 Wordwise: The bag

After, when, but, but, So, because, Although, When/As soon as, because, and, So, and, After, and, and

2 Wordwise: if or when

When, if, If, if, when, if, if, if, If

3 Wordwise: Weather report

Lösungsvorschlag:
On Tuesday it will rain in the north of Scotland. Temperatures will be around 13°C.
It will be cloudy and windy in the south of Scotland and north England. Temperatures will be around 15°C.
The heart of England (Midlands) and Wales will see some sun/clouds. Temperatures will be around 17°C.
The south of England will be sunny all day. It will be warmer than in other parts of Britain.

4 Language: Where is my lunchbox?

hers, mine, his, his, hers, mine, theirs, yours, Ours

5 Language: The purse

the owner will be very unhappy; if we keep all the money, If the owner comes back; if we leave the purse under the tree; the police will know what to do; the happy owner will give us something as a 'thank you'

6 Language: A rainy weekend

will, are going to, won't, will, will, is going to, are going to, won't, are going to

Green Line 2
Vorschläge zur Leistungsmessung
ISBN: 978-3-12-560016-4

Unit 7 English everywhere

1 Wordwise: Travel words

airport: flight, plane, to take off, terminal, bus, helicopter, to land, customs, announcement
harbour: ferry, terminal, ship, coast, sea, ocean, customs, announcement
station: shuttle, platform, train, announcement
what people take on trips: passport, baggage, map

2 Wordwise: Verbs

a) bleed – bled – bled; break – broke – broken; call – called – called; eat – ate – eaten; fight – fought – fought; hide – hid – hidden; hit – hit – hit; miss – missed – missed; ride – rode – ridden; shake – shook – shaken; speak – spoke – spoken; send – sent – sent;

b) *Individuelle S-Antwort*

3 Language: Be polite

1. Could/Can 2. May/Can/Could 3. May/Shall 4. May/Could/Can 5. May/Can; shall 6. Could/Can; couldn't; shouldn't/needn't

4 Language: A project

have always done; told; picked up; thought; hasn't been; has just started; looked; found

5 Language: After the first day

Lösungsvorschlag:
Did your classmates show/tell you where to go?
– Yes, they did.
Did your teacher/classmates ask for your name?
– Yes, he/she/they did.
Did your teacher give you any homework?
– No, he didn't.
Did anyone talk to you? – Yes, some pupils did.
Did anyone take you home? – No, I took the bus.
Did anyone meet/welcome you? – Yes, my teacher met me at the entrance.
Did anyone have lunch with you? – Yes, some of my classmates.
Did you get any homework? – No, I didn't.

6 Language: The fortune-teller

Lösungsvorschlag:
What will my brother do?
– He'll work with computers in Scotland.
How many children will I have? – Five.
When will I be famous? – In 2025.
Where will I live? – You'll live in a small village.
Who will have a nice house?
– You and your family will have a nice house.
Why will I drive a small car?
– Because you won't need a big one.
How many birthday presents will I get?
– You won't get many. Maybe two, but they will be big ones.
Will my friends give me a dog for my birthday?
– No, they won't. They'll give you a black cat.

7 Language: An interview

1. Have you ever been to Germany to make a film? 2. Have you ever read other vampire stories? 3. Have you ever needed a stuntman? 4. Have you ever forgotten your text and said something funny? 5. Have you ever performed on stage in a theatre?

Green Line 2
Vorschläge zur Leistungsmessung
ISBN: 978-3-12-560016-4

Green Line 2
Vorschläge zur Leistungsmessung
ISBN: 978-3-12-560016-4

Hörverstehenstexte zu den Vorschlägen zur Leistungsmessung

Track	Unit	Text/Übungstitel	Seite	Übung	Spielzeit
1	1	Listening: Back at school	3	1	1'44"
2	1	Listening: Big trouble	3	2	1'39"
3	1	Extra listening: A phone call to grandma	Zusatz	Extra	1'56"
4	2	Listening: A day out in London	8	1	1'44"
5	2	Listening: A trip to London	8	2	1'55"
6	2	Extra listening: A phone call	Zusatz	Extra	2'20"
7	3	Listening: Shopping at the supermarket	13	1	2'34"
8	3	Listening: Pocket money ideas	13	2	1'49"
9	3	Extra listening: At Street Style	Zusatz	Extra	3'24"
10	4	Listening: Robbie Williams	18	1	2'57"
11	4	Listening: Stars and their prizes	18	2	1'52"
12	4	Extra listening: An audition	Zusatz	Extra	2'03"
13	5	Listening: Is it the same everywhere?	23	1	2'43"
14	5	Listening: At the hospital	23	2	1'57"
15	5	Extra listening: Stop that!	Zusatz	Extra	1'20"
16	6	Listening: A weekend in Scotland	28	1	2'01"
17	6	Listening: Weekend plans	28	2	1'54"
18	6	Extra listening: Clichés	Zusatz	Extra	2'12"
19	7	Listening: Going abroad	33	1	3'16"
20	7	Listening: At the travel agent's	33	2	3'41"
21	7	Extra listening: At the reception	Zusatz	Extra	2'08"

Gesamtspielzeit: 47'33"

ISBN: 978-3-12-560016-4

Lehrersoftware-CD

Empfohlene Systemvoraussetzungen:

- PC mit 500 MHz oder höher
- Windows 2000, XP, Vista (32 bit), 7
- 512 MB RAM
- S-VGA-kompatible Grafikkarte mit 16,7 Mio Farben (24 bit)
- mind. 50 MB bis max. 200 MB freier Speicherplatz bei Kopie der Medien auf die Festplatte
- 24fach CD-ROM-Laufwerk
- Bildschirmauflösung (Programm) 800 x 600 Pixel
- Schwarzweiß- oder Farbdrucker mit 300 dpi Druckauflösung
- Microsoft Word (ab Version 2000) oder OpenOffice (ab Version 2.0)

Schnellstart der Software:

Die Installation kopiert das Programm auf die Festplatte Ihres Rechners. Wir empfehlen, die Medien sofort auf die Festplatte zu installieren. Sie brauchen dann die CD-ROM nicht mehr einzulegen, um das Programm zu verwenden.

- Legen Sie die Lehrersoftware CD in Ihr CD-ROM-Laufwerk ein.
- Die Autostartfunktion öffnet ein Fenster mit dem Inhalt der CD-ROM.
- Starten Sie die Datei „SETUP.EXE" durch Doppelklick und folgen Sie den Anweisungen, um das Programm und die Medien auf Ihre Festplatte zu installieren.
- Um das Programm zu installieren, müssen Sie dem Lizenzvertrag zustimmen (s.a. Lizenz.txt auf der CD-ROM).
- Den Pfad für die Programminstallation auf der Festplatte können Sie anpassen oder nach der Vorgabe übernehmen. Wenn Sie bereits Green Line Lehrersoftware installiert haben, muss die Installation in dasselbe Verzeichnis erfolgen.
- Sie starten das Programm über Start – Programme – Klett – Green Line – Lehrersoftware Green Line oder über das Icon auf Ihrem Desktop.

Bitte beachten:
Wenn Sie bereits Green Line Standardaufgaben Ausgabe Niedersachsen besitzen, achten Sie bitte bei der Installation darauf, dass Sie zuerst die Standardaufgaben Niedersachsen installieren und danach die Green Line Vorschläge zur Leistungsmessung.
Wir empfehlen, die Installationsreihenfolge – erst Standardaufgaben, dann Vorschläge zur Leistungsmessung – auch einzuhalten, wenn Sie bereits Standardaufgaben Green Line Bundesausgabe besitzen.

Auf der CD-ROM befindet sich ein ausführliches Handbuch zum Programm.

Green Line 2
Vorschläge zur Leistungsmessung
ISBN: 978-3-12-560016-4